Elevate Your Life

Elevate Your Life

Crafting Your Life's Masterpiece
Through Your Decisions

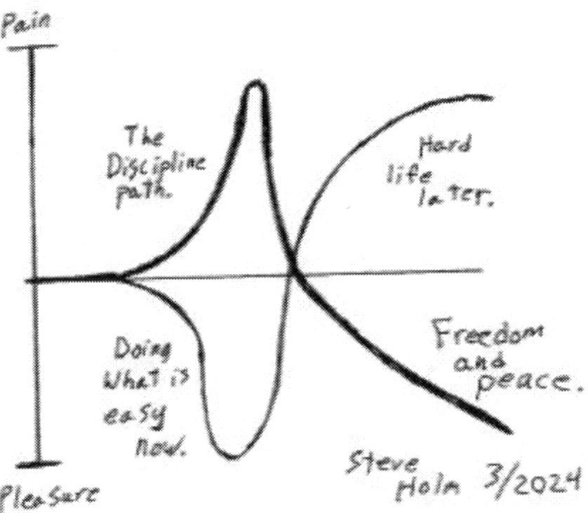

Steve Holm

ISBN: 979-8-89525-012-9

Contents

Introduction

Picture a standard homemade meal. Something filling, not flashy—meat, vegetable, starch. Sure, it's something that you'd eat, but you're not exactly going wild for it. You might take a bite of the protein, pick at the veggies, or just tuck as much of the food as you can into your napkin to sneak to your dog later.

Now, imagine that you've been lost for three days without anything to eat or drink. Suddenly, that simple chicken/broccoli/rice combo looks so extremely good that you'd have to force yourself to stop short of biting the plate.

The food was the same. You were different.

Your level of hunger affects your appetite. If you were hungry enough, you might even find that the things that were once a little hard to swallow now seemed mouthwatering. Without the hunger? You'd probably decline the meal even if it were given to you for free.

This teaches us the first step to getting what you want: you have to *really* want it.

As you embark on your journey of personal improvement, the first thing you need to cultivate is a different kind of hunger. There's no book you can read that will do you any good unless you're willing to open your mind and consider new perspectives. You'll need to be hungry to learn new things, to analyze your habits, and to expand your mind—even if it means you have to confront uncomfortable truths, face your faults, and embrace new challenges. As the name implies, even self-growth has its share of growing pains. Only the hungry people will be able to push through them.

If you're reading this book, you and I are fueled by the same hunger. Hungry people seek success like a shark that smells blood in the water. People who are hungry have a drive to understand, evaluate, and elevate themselves. They're not content to watch on the sidelines as life passes them by. They're only happy if they're sitting in the driver's seat. That's why hunger is the defining momentum that separates the winners from the crowd.

Hunger is the first step. But hunger without direction is just obsession. Plenty of people are hungry, but they don't reflect on the root of their hunger. In the search for fulfillment, they might get into drugs and alcohol—or simply try to fill the void with more innocuous habits, like excessive gaming or retail therapy. Stuffing ourselves with these sugary fillers is just a way to mask a hunger for something real and extraordinary.

If you're reading this book, you're ready to focus your hunger away from easy junk food (AKA, negative habits) to nutrient-dense meals that will actually fill you up (positive change). It's time to develop a craving for real growth. A hunger for professional, personal, educational, and spiritual growth is the key to self-improvement. That's why this book is about identifying and harnessing hunger and using it to propel yourself in the right direction. It's the biggest motivating force for any learning journey. It leads to constant improvement and continual growth. If you maintain this drive, it will ultimately lead you to success.

Luckily, this type of hunger is something that can be nurtured. We're all responsible for building this drive within ourselves. It requires us to adjust our view of life, commit to difficult change, and convert our hunger into discipline. That's what this book is for.

Imagine a graph that depicts the history of a stock exchange. As different circumstances affect the company, the value of the stock rises and falls over time, with some prolonged plateaus or valleys.

Now, rather than the value of a stock, imagine a line graph that represents the quality of your life. Pull out a piece of paper and create a vertical axis and horizontal axis. The horizontal axis represents time. For this exercise, limit the horizontal axis to the past 5 years. The vertical axis represents the quality of your life. Use this graph to draw a rough line that depicts how the quality of your life has gone up and down over the course of that time.

Let's take a look at your highest and lowest points. Reflect on what happened in your life to cause these changes. How did you come back from your lowest moments? How did you contribute to your biggest successes?

I devised this visualization—called a life graph—to demonstrate how our decisions impact our lives. As you look over your life graph, try to identify past actions that have led to upward and downward trends. Then, imagine what you want your life graph to look like five years from now. Even with its dips and falls, your life graph should always be climbing to the top. A good life is about promoting the upward trajectory while minimizing the negativity. After 30 years of living an empowered life, you'd be able to zoom out on that graph and find a mountain of progress separating you from where you started.

As I developed this concept, I recognized an important fact: our current choices create our futures. If we want to live better tomorrow, we have to make the best choices today.

Per day, we make about 35,000 decisions. From what shoes we wear to how we interact with others, these decisions add up to create the direction of our lives. Even our small decisions lead to a positive or negative impact, whether it's in our personal lives or professional careers. For example, picking up this book may be a small action, but it could be the very beginning of an upward trajectory. There's power in making just one of our 35,000 decisions a powerful and purposeful choice.

Welcome to *Elevate Your Life*

I'm a young and simple thinker, but I have a hunger for learning, growing, and achieving my dreams. At the age of 15, I committed myself to being a student of leadership. Years ago, I realized that there's no faster way to learn life's lessons than taking notes from those who already had what I wanted. Ever since then, I've spent my time reading about experts in life, relationships, and business.

Think of this book as a beginner's guide to self-improvement. If you're starting to explore the wide world of personal growth, business advice, and self-help, the sheer bulk of available content can be overwhelming. Between hundreds of books, biographies, and documentaries—not to mention thousands of videos and blogs worth of online content—it's a challenge just to figure out where to start on your personal journey. That's why I've compiled essential concepts that provide a foundation for self-improvement to fuel your future research.

We'll address vital topics like setting goals, maintaining health, and prioritizing self-improvement. On the way, we're going to talk about everything from finding personal fulfillment to finding the right credit card. *Elevate Your Life* isn't meant to be a compilation of my opinions on these important subjects. Instead, my goal is to open your mind up to new perspectives. Turn these ideas over in your mind, compare them with your current beliefs, and test them in your future research and personal experiences. If you're willing to maintain this open-minded perspective, I believe you'll find life-changing information in this book. I hope *Elevate Your Life* will work to boost your energy, spark a fire in you, and encourage you to formulate a dream for your life—and a plan on how to make it a reality.

The concepts in *Elevate Your Life* are designed to be accessible and approachable. Anyone who is looking to improve their personal, spiritual, and financial well-being can use the information in this book. It's not just for prospective business owners—it's for parents and students, grunt-workers and managers. No matter what previous experience you bring to the table, this book can help you improve on your current talents, increase your capacity, and level up your mindset.

A Guide to *Elevate Your Life*

One of my goals with this book was to create a handbook to the incredible resources that have influenced my life journey so far. Since I want to encourage independent research into these topics, I've included in-depth references throughout this book. I've also added reference lists with recommended reading at the end of most chapters.

You'll also find several inspiring stories, including some of my own personal experiences. These stories highlight some of the most important messages in this book.

Elevate Your Life begins by laying the foundations of personal growth. This process starts by becoming self-aware. My first chapters focus on developing a positive attitude and maintaining beneficial habits. We're going to discuss ways to identify personal goals, define a powerful strategy, and maintain momentum. In the second half of this book, I outline some of the most relevant self-improvement concepts, including finances and personal health.

To make this reading experience effective, I recommend treating it like a travel guide. Keep a notebook nearby to jot down main ideas that stick with you; screenshot quotes that resonate with your experiences; take note of references that you want to check out or topics that you want to research later. As you read, try to find your three favorite spots in the book and bookmark them for future reference. Later, when you're knee-deep in your personal journey, you can easily return to these spots to get encouraged and recentered.

To encourage you to save and share your favorite parts of this book, I'm setting up a giveaway. Simply tag @steveholmbooks on Instagram with a picture of the quote or lesson that you liked best, along with a photo of this book's cover. Once you've posted, you'll be entered into the giveaway, where you'll have the chance to win a free copy of the book to share with a friend, loved one, or boss who really needs to learn a thing or two.

As we begin, I want to remind you to center your thoughts on what you want. You won't become exceptionally healthy by eating the average diet. You won't beat the morning rush by waking up at the average time. If you put in average actions, you'll never get exceptional results. The world is ready for more leaders in business, in health, and in life. Our life is how we lead it, and it will become what we shape it.

Let's start setting an above-average trend that will reshape our life graph and inspire those around us.

The two most important things to our lives are progress and direction. We're not trying to be perfect—we're just trying to keep the line of our life graph always pointing upward. If we're in the mindset of constant improvement, we will continue to be elevated every day.

CHAPTER 1

Elevating Mindset

"The greatest discovery of my generation is that a human being can alter his life by altering his attitude of mind."

—William James

If you could sell a positive mindset in a bottle, the tagline would be:

"Tired of dealing with negativity and low morale? Looking for a motivating environment that promotes productivity? Look no further! Introducing the power of positive attitudes."

One of the greatest secrets to self-growth is seizing control of your life through your mindset. Your mindset is how you see what happens to you. It defines your attitude, which is the approach you have to everyday life and the way you present yourself to others around you. These two terms will be used interchangeably throughout this book.

In many ways, attitude controls your life. A good attitude empowers you to look to the future and make more balanced, honest decisions—while negative attitudes hold you back by preventing you from seeing and seizing opportunities.

Imagine someone cutting you off in traffic. They veer into your lane three feet from your bumper without any turn signal to be seen. In this scenario, you can calmly brake to let them in and carry on, or you can get frustrated, honk your horn, and swerve around them. You can either let it go, or you can spend the rest of the drive fuming about the reckless driver. In one instance, the negative experience rolled off of you—in the other, *you* held onto *it*.

By responding negatively to this experience, you give the reckless driver control over you. If you were stuck in a negative mindset, you could be mentally cut off in traffic for the rest of the day. Negative responses to negative experiences make roadblocks. On the other hand, positivity swerves.

Mindset is the lens through which you interpret the events of your life. In this way, your mindset is responsible for assigning meaning. When your friend gives you a rain check, your instinct may be to call them a flake. This negative mindset interprets the meaning of your friend's action as an insult or a reflection on their character flaws. However, if you decide to approach the situation with a positive mindset, you might consider underlying causes. Maybe your friend has been stressed at work, or they're dealing with family troubles. The meaning changes the exchange from an insult to an opportunity. Now, you have the chance to provide support and strengthen your connection.

So, mindset = meaning, which affects action. On a larger scale, this means your mindset interprets the very meaning of your life's circumstances. When difficult situations arise, some interpret the meaning negatively. It's a common response to hardship; they feel like God is punishing them. What would happen if, instead, they adopted a positive mindset? Suddenly, the challenging situation becomes an opportunity to grow, a necessary step towards actualization and self-understanding. The problem becomes a gift from God. Your mindset alone has the power to change a punishment into a blessing.

This positive mindset doesn't just make you a happier person—it also shifts your attention away from wallowing and towards problem-solving. Instead of blaming your friend for their bad habits, you can offer them a helping hand. Instead of bashing on your greater power for life's tragedies, you can grow from your experiences. Instead of crashing into the reckless driver, you can keep traffic running smoothly.

Only you can make these choices. Winston Churchill has a famous quote: "Attitude is a little thing that makes a big difference." In my life, I've translated this to: "If attitude is everything, then put everything into your attitude."

The Creator Mentality

Tony Robbins, an influential self-help coach that we'll discuss a lot in this book, hosts a yearly conference called Unleash the Power Within (UPW). The 2022 UPW conference featured Nick Santonastasso, an inspirational keynote speaker, fitness model, and author. At his presentation, Nick spoke about a difficult choice that his parents had to make. They had to decide whether or not they were going to abort him.

Nick was born with Hanhart syndrome, which prevented his limbs from fully growing, leaving him with one arm and no legs. In spite of his challenges, Nick has lived an extraordinary life, and he remains widely known for his upbeat messages and optimistic thinking. In his UPW speech, Nick said, "In your life, there are two identities that you can step into. You can either be the victim, or you can be the victor."

The victim mentality keeps you permanently in the passenger seat of your life. As a victim, you don't have control over where you came from, and you're unable control where you're going. Victims watch as challenges rush towards them, paralyzed and unable to turn.

A positive mindset frees you of the victim mentality. Everyone has challenges. We can either avoid these challenges by blaming our circumstances, or we can conquer them by becoming the architect of our future. That's why I prefer my slight variation on Nick's phrase: you can either be a victim, or you can be a creator.

When I was nine years old, my father left my family. By the time I was ten, I realized that I was responsible for filling some of the empty hole he left behind. There was a sense that if I didn't take care of my mother, no one else would. This was when I switched from the mindset of victim to the mindset of a creator.

Since then, I've spent my life trying to make a better life for my siblings and my mother. As I grew into adulthood, I realized that this experience required what was ultimately a rewarding shift in my mindset. I couldn't change the fact that my father left when I was at such a young age. It was a negative thing that happened to me that I had no control over—but I could choose to respond in a way that made the experience a net positive.

This mentality is how I keep my negative impulses in check. I have chosen to live a life of creation instead of victimization. While I can't change my past mistakes, the circumstances of my childhood, and the opportunities that I wasn't born into, I can shape my life from where I'm standing, right now. You cannot control your family or your genetic tendencies. Blaming your parents for these challenges will never solve them. Instead, a positive mentality converts the time you would have spent complaining into energy that you can use to create.

By shedding the victim mentality, you empower yourself to create a healthy, happy, and balanced future. It's time to put aside the victim mentality and become the creators of our futures. This is a secret to breaking free of your self-limiting beliefs and conquering your critical inner voice.

When I was fifteen, I decided I wanted to own a truck. I was committed. I told myself that I wouldn't let anything stop me. I expected others to tell me "You're too young," and I decided ahead of time that it would be my goal to prove them wrong. With this determined, positive mindset, I bought my $4,500 Toyota Tacoma. At 15, I was too young to drive it legally. I spent hours of free time earning money to pay off my car loan so that, after getting my license, I'd be able to drive it debt-free.

One year later, I bought a 2006 Duramax for $24,000. I remember that my uncles were impressed that I managed it at sixteen years old. They'd said, "That's not an average sixteen-year-old boy. He's proven he can achieve something far beyond his years."

At that moment, I realized the satisfaction of having a positive mindset. As a young person, it can often feel like life is out of reach. No matter your age, mastering your mindset is a worthwhile effort that you can make for your future. Focus on what you can do, not what you can't do. This will be the springboard that gets you where you want to be. As Marcus Aurelius said, "Our life is what our thoughts make it."

Positive Karma

Sometimes, life breaks the rules. When it comes to positivity, opposites do not attract.

When you foster positivity within yourself, you repel negativity.

People who are positive attract other positive people—and positive people are usually the ones who are getting things done. It's like a ticket into the room where the big decisions happen.

Positivity can also affect the environment around you. Negativity will never lift up negativity—but positivity can always bring encouragement and engagement to a negative situation. Your mindset is a big factor in determining your day-to-day performance. With a good mindset, you can more easily build trust and loyalty among colleagues. Approaching challenges with a positive mindset creates an inclusive work environment. Increased communication, cooperation, and innovation are direct results of this shared mindset. Positive mindsets eliminate missed opportunities and cut out unnecessary drama, whether it's at your job or in your personal relationships.

In one word, a positive mindset sets karma into motion. What you do to other people, good or bad, will come around in your life. Your positivity brings more positivity.

A positive mindset attracts people to inspire you—meanwhile, a negative attitude seeks out negative people to relate to. Karma goes both ways. Negativity certainly harms those around you, but, importantly, it wears down on your sense of self. This can lead you into harmful self-doubt. A person's mindset shapes their beliefs about themselves. Those with negative mindsets don't exclude themselves from the negativity. They cast their own limits close by because they don't believe they could ever reach the finish line. This is how your mindset affects your goals.

The direction of your thoughts is the direction of your feet—you'll find that you end up wherever you were thinking. This means that a negative mindset will keep you fixated on a negative future.

Keeping a positive mindset isn't about ignoring the negativity in your life. Instead, it's about choosing to be optimistic in the midst of difficulty. Ignorance pretends the road is level. Positivity inspires you to push through the rough terrain. Take a moment to think about a negative experience that affected you. How would the experience be different if you had decided that it was going to shape you for the better? This is the power of positivity.

Positive attitudes often resolve problems big and small. By simply believing in creative solutions, you're far more likely to find them. With a positive attitude, nothing in the world can stop you from being powerful. Even through failure, positivity breeds new opportunities. In a business setting, customers are attracted to positive people. Creative and enthusiastic employees with solution-oriented thinking can be the difference between a one-time customer and a loyal advocate for your business. A team with a positive mindset will bounce back, find unique solutions, and learn from setbacks.

In your personal life, positivity will encourage you to adapt to change and stay on course despite difficult situations or toxic influences. Think back to the ups and downs of your life graph. Remember positivity can't always reduce the downs, but it does stabilize you in times of struggle. There's no better way to create a sense of resilience than strengthening your mindset. Your mindset can turn the sticks and stones that were thrown at you into building materials for your future.

I believe that by intentionally cultivating a positive mindset, your life will become as happy as you want it to be. In your mind, you have the power to dictate your success, health, and happiness.

Shaping Your Mindset

Now that we understand the power of our mindsets, let's discuss actionable ways to develop positivity.

It can be difficult to create a positive mental environment when you are inundated with negativity. In our current digital age, social media is a massive source of daily negativity. If you're ready to make a meaningful change, take a look at your follow list on your favorite social media platform. Is there anyone on your list who spreads negativity? Who do you follow that actively highlights the positive side of life?

In my personal life, I have purposefully subscribed to positive people and unsubscribed from negative people. If someone isn't working to make the world a better place, I can simply click a button to unsubscribe from their content. It's the easiest negative influence to remove. No need to waste energy spreading harmful talk about them—the most surefire way to destroy a negative person's publicity is to avoid talking about them completely.

Additionally, be sure to reflect on your personal connections. Your friends and family have a significant influence on your life. Without even realizing it, you may be allowing them to drastically affect your mindset. If you find yourself surrounded by negative people, consider ways that you might reach out to positive influences that you admire.

I have experienced many negative influences in my life. Negative people love to make more people negative. When I began my career in real estate, many of my personal friends discouraged me from taking it on. They warned me I wouldn't be able to make money—that I was wasting my time. I remember thanking them for their advice, shaking their hands, and then leaving to chase after my vision for my future. I read books, found video guides, and studied in-depth information to find what I'd need to know to succeed. Within a year, I owned my own house.

It wasn't that my friends were being unkind or didn't believe in me. They were giving me advice based on their personal mindset. When I stuck with my positive vision, I found that I was able to overcome the things they imagined were impossible.

Chris Do, life coach, YouTuber, and founder of online education platform *The Futur*, has taught that our circumstances cannot define who we become. At the 2019 American Institute of Graphic Arts Design Conference, Chris spoke about people with successful habits. "A lot of times, we think that it must be because they were born with it, or it was something else," he said. "As a teacher, it doesn't help me to believe that you are born with it. So, I have to believe that you must be able to learn this."

Chris was consulting a mechanical engineer and graphic designer who was hitting a glass ceiling in her earnings. She turned to Chris for advice. Six months later, she'd already made more than she had the previous year. She hadn't changed the services that she'd offered. She'd simply adjusted her mindset about her work, the quality of her work, and the compensation that she was determined to receive. From this experience, Chris shares a secret formula to living a positive mindset: "The thing that you need to do is to believe *and then do it*."

You have 24 hours in the day. Out of those, you have about sixteen waking hours. When you wake up in the morning, make a commitment to spend four of those sixteen hours without any negativity in your mindset. Stick to this goal. If negativity creeps in, use the tips that we've discussed in this chapter to recenter your mindset.

Once you can spend four hours of your day without negativity, up your goal to eight. In the long-term, your objective is to spend every day focusing more on the good than the bad. Once you've developed positivity as a habit, you'll notice that your detrimental mindset begins to fade away completely, leaving you with a positive mental voice.

Developing a positive mindset is fundamental to self-growth. Feel free to dive into this concept further through the resources included at the end of this chapter, and don't forget to use the internet to find information that is more relevant to your journey.

Overcoming Challenges

In their book *Success Through a Positive Mental Attitude,* authors Napoleon Hill and W. Clement Stone present a valuable guide to developing a positive mindset. The secret? Think of your problems as nothing more than opportunities.

Disappointments are the best: the bigger, the better. Disappointment gives you an opportunity to overcome. When you think this way, you don't give up after the first failed attempt. Positive mindsets turn bankruptcies from hardships into signs that you're one step closer to success. Think of these setbacks as a new beginning—the start of an exciting chapter.

I've dealt with countless situations in my life where it seemed like everything was going downhill. When I bought my first house, I hired a property management company. The representative toured the house and began to list off all of the problems with the property. He told me it wasn't worth the money, and that he wouldn't be able to rent it out. I kept waiting for him to shift away from criticism and start offering me proactive solutions. I wanted him to describe the changes that would improve the property or highlight the priority projects that we could complete to increase the house's market value. Instead, he was set on abandoning the property.

At that moment, I knew I'd have to figure it out on my own. I asked the rep to leave the property, and then I started planning. I could have put the house up for sale and abandoned my original plan to use it as a rental property. But, instead, I choose to stick with it and overcome the challenges instead of wallowing in them.

Let's consider the honeybee.

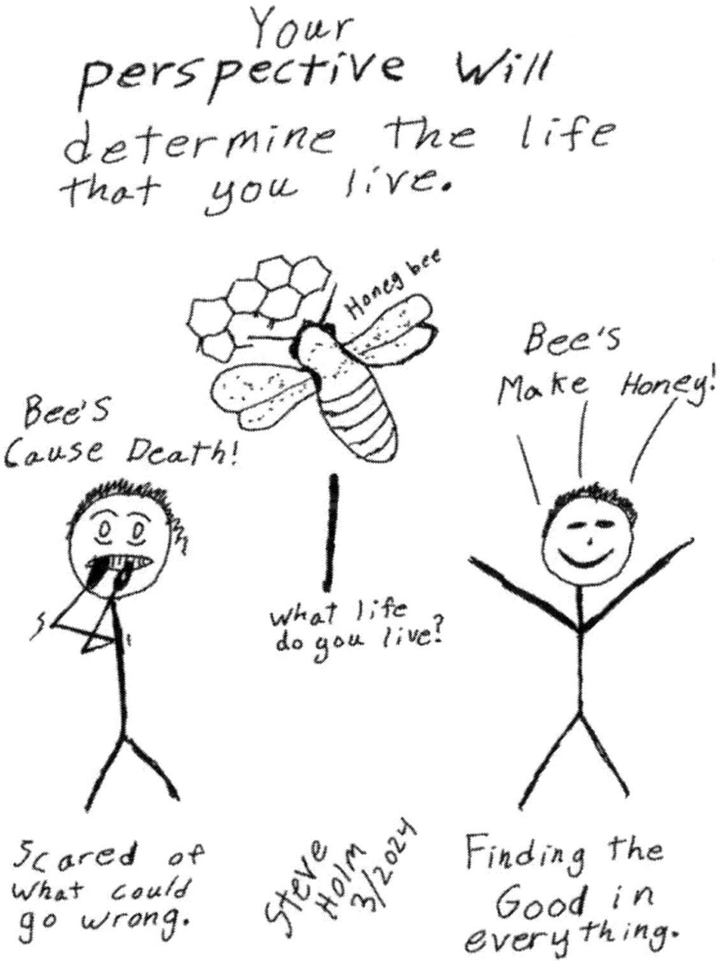

Some people live their life afraid of honeybees. They see them as a threat. Bees mean bee stings. For those with an allergy, bees are an omen of death. These people are petrified by everything that could go wrong. This fear could cause them to lash out, run away, or attack the bee—which only makes it more likely that they'll get stung.

On the other side, someone with a positive mindset might see honeybees in a different light. Bees make honey. They pollinate gardens. This person doesn't freak out when a bee crosses their path. Instead, they find the good in everything. This keeps them calm, collected, and happy.

When I was fifteen years old, I read Robert Kiyosaki and Sharon Lechter's *Rich Dad Poor Dad.* In one simple concept, Robert and Sharon defined the mindset that you need to have to succeed. They said, "Ask yourself how you can afford it instead of telling yourself that you can't afford it."

Since I've adopted this mindset, I've found incredible stores of personal resilience. I've made things that have completely flopped, business deals that have gone totally sidewise. Yet, whether it was a batch of cookies I've burned in the oven or a machine I couldn't get to work, it never took me long to get back on my feet and try again. I had decided that I wasn't going to let anything stop me. In practice, a good mindset keeps you on track. It becomes an endless conversation that talks you away from dark places and discouragement. As Jocko Willink, a retired Navy SEAL and podcaster, said. "You can give up, stand down, take off your gear, and quit. Or you can mourn the loss, celebrate the life, lock and load your weapons, and you can go do what you're supposed to do. I choose to go get some."

References for Future Learning

Rich Dad Poor Dad by Robert Kiyosaki and Sharon Lechter

Success Through a Positive Mental Attitude by Napoleon Hill and W. Clement Stone

The Futur, a YouTube Channel by Chris Do

Victim to Victor: How to Overcome Victim Mentality to Live the Life You Love by Nick Santonastasso

CHAPTER 2

Changing Perspective

"Whatever the mind of man can conceive and believe, the mind of man can achieve."

—Napoleon Hill

Everyone has their own perspective. We wear our perspective like a pair of sunglasses. It colors everything that happens in our lives. We can't escape it. However, we do have the power to try new perspectives on for size. Changing your perspective is about seeing things from a different angle. It allows us to break free from limitations and it expands our view of the future. When we regularly change out our perspective sunglasses, we're more likely to see the world for how it actually is and develop a greater idea of the bigger picture. On the other hand, if we stick with the same pair of sunglasses our entire life, there are shades of color that we'll never see.

Switching up our sunglasses is valuable, but it isn't always comfortable. Sometimes, developing the right perspective requires you to sacrifice your personal feelings.

Let's say you get the car of your dreams. It has all the features you'd ever want—tinted windows, spotless rims, customized paint job. You work for months to pay off the loan, adjusting your budget or working odd jobs on the side to make extra payments. The day you get the loan paid off, you celebrate by giving it a total detailing. It's a squeaky-clean dream come true.

On the way home from the car wash, someone rear-ends you.

Here's where perspective comes into play. The car was your baby—you've poured hours of effort into it. It's a direct product of your hard work. Seeing the situation through your natural perspective, it can feel like your life has literally just ended.

Consider a different view. Take a step back. Car accidents happen all the time. Often, they result in lifelong injuries or fatalities. Every day, we travel at high speeds in heavy machinery that has the potential to *literally* end a life. Yes, the car will be expensive to fix—but, miraculously, no one was hurt. Compared to a human life, a rear-ended car—even a beloved rear-ended car—becomes very small.

This is a common example of a fundamental truth: we're all a part of a larger picture. When we set our experiences in context, we're able to remain motivated and solution-oriented.

Improve Your Clarity

Let's revisit the glasses metaphor. Consider how your specific brand of sunglasses filter the world around you. What is your perspective in life and in your relationships? What do you pay attention to? Are you focused on the little stuff, or are you locked on the big picture?

Every perspective has blind spots. Without even knowing it, your glasses may be scratched, damaged, or dirty. Think about an experience you've had where your perspective has limited you. There were things that you weren't able to see, whether it was because you were too centered on yourself, on small details, or on negative experiences.

New perspectives make room for new revelations. When you change perspectives, you see solutions that were hiding behind the problems. This is why we all benefit from getting in the habit of switching out our lenses. It helps us see the world clearly.

A balanced perspective also improves our understanding of our life choices. It allows us to zoom out on our life graph (see Chapter 1) and identify where we are today. Perspective lets us take an honest look at our past and see where our current decisions will take us in the future.

The ability to shift perspective is what allows us to prioritize internal achievement over external validation. When our perspective focuses on our internal efforts instead of our external successes, we can find self-fulfillment, even in challenging circumstances. On the other hand, when we get mired in a single, negative perspective of life, we can be surrounded by achievements yet fail to find happiness.

The Value of a Balanced Perspective

Being able to shift your perspective is a vital skill for both professional and personal success. In the workplace, front-line workers can easily get burnt out. They often have little job satisfaction. Even if they work for daring companies with exciting visions, they feel limited to a seemingly small job. Yet, when we zoom out a little bit, we find that front-line workers are often the backbone of customer relations and production. They're an integral part of a larger environment that would crumble without them.

Realizing that you are a part of something bigger encourages you. Simply understanding that you're an important member in a team can increase your participation and your long-term investment. In turn, this understanding of the big picture can improve the quality of your work. For all you front-line workers out there, consider ways that you can be a proactive problem-solving to reduce strain in the big picture, and you'll find that you get noticed.

For upper-level administrators, maintaining a larger perspective allows you to work more effectively. I've seen many managers fall into the same trap. They get caught up in the small details. When you're obsessed with the little stuff, the big picture can get lost. I once had an opportunity to work under a wonderful manager. I felt that he was extremely smart and able to quickly solve problems—but he couldn't stop himself from wasting his time on the smallest tasks. As a result, he worked more hours than anyone else and still ran out of time to finish what he had to do for that day. Our team wanted to look to him for direction on the vision of the company, but he wasn't able to strategize at the top level. At the end of the day, it cost the company a lot of wasted time and effort. Big problems would build up over weeks because he was centered on the small details instead of the big picture.

On a personal level, the ability to shift perspectives allows you to connect with others. Let's say you get in an argument with a loved one. If you're committed exclusively to your perspective, you automatically limit yourself. From your perspective, there's only one way to understand the other person's actions. When you're able to detach yourself from your opinions and look at the situation from a different perspective, you're able to acknowledge the good points from both parties. You can better understand the motivations of the other person and even identify the emotions that may be motivating both sides of the argument. When you shift perspectives in this way, you increase your sense of nuance and maturity while fostering better communication.

Shifting perspective is vital to solving personal miscommunication. I believe that misunderstanding is the first cause of dissatisfaction in any relationship. When you are stuck in your perspective, you talk to others the way that you would talk to yourself. You send cues that you would pick up on and use language that you would understand. Yet you're not communicating with yourself—you're trying to connect with another person. For a dramatic example of this, consider trying to explain an advanced math problem to a toddler. Unless you try to explain something through their perspective, they will never be able to understand.

By changing your perspective to the individual that you're speaking to, you can adjust the way you communicate to make it more effective. It also forces you to release preconceived notions and biases that you may have had about the other person. When you're both willing to consider the others' perspective, you can approach the relationship with an open mind and grow together. This works for coworkers, employees, spouses, siblings, parents and children. When you're willing to "put themselves in their shoes" and see the world through their eyes, you make it easier to communicate and connect.

In this chapter, I've offered some of the foundational basics for shifting perspective and building relationships through understanding. We've only scratched the surface. There are dozens of resources readily available online that expand on these ideas in-depth.

Making Change

Your mindset, your attitude, and your perspective work together to define the way that you see yourself in the big picture. Like your mindset, your perspective can be a source of negativity or positivity in your life. You may find that you're stuck behind an old pair of glasses that tell you you can't do it. Your perspective is centered on your negative qualities, on your challenges, and, worst of all, on your past mistakes.

You do not deserve to see your life through that lens. It's time to get fitted for an uplifting new perspective that focuses on how to make things happen. You are not limited by your circumstances. Nothing is out of your reach.

Don't believe me? Think of everything you have that holds you back. I'll bet it will take one internet search to find someone who made success with all of your challenges and more.

There's a big four-letter word that we too often see side-by-side with *success*.

It's *luck*.

From the traditional perspective, luck is a sign that the universe loves you. In my eyes, luck is the intersection where opportunity meets willingness. Everyone can get on the road and find that intersection. By preparing on a personal level, researching, and reflecting on yourself, you'll find that you meet luck pretty quickly.

Instead of waiting for luck to find you, go and find it. This is the perspective that will drive you to succeed.

CHAPTER 3

Setting and Reassessing Goals

"The best way to predict the future is to create it."

—Peter Drucker

When you're navigating with a map, you can't progress until you identify two crucial things: 1. Where you are, and 2. Where you want to be. People who lack the first are confused—people who lack the second are directionless. If a traveler doesn't have a name for their destination, no road will ever take them there. It's like playing darts without knowing what a bullseye looks like.

In the first two chapters of this book, we discussed the role of mindset and perspective in how you view the world and who you are within that world. Now, it's time to develop a sense of who you want to be. In this chapter, we're going to work on translating dreams into detailed goals.

The difference between a "dream" and a "goal" is in the details. Wanting a clean house is a dream; wanting a clean living room, a clean kitchen, clean bedrooms, and clean bathrooms is a goal. As you develop plans to reach your goals, they become more detailed, and, through that process, more plausible. Imagine putting your dreams through a refiner's fire. Goals are what come out the other side.

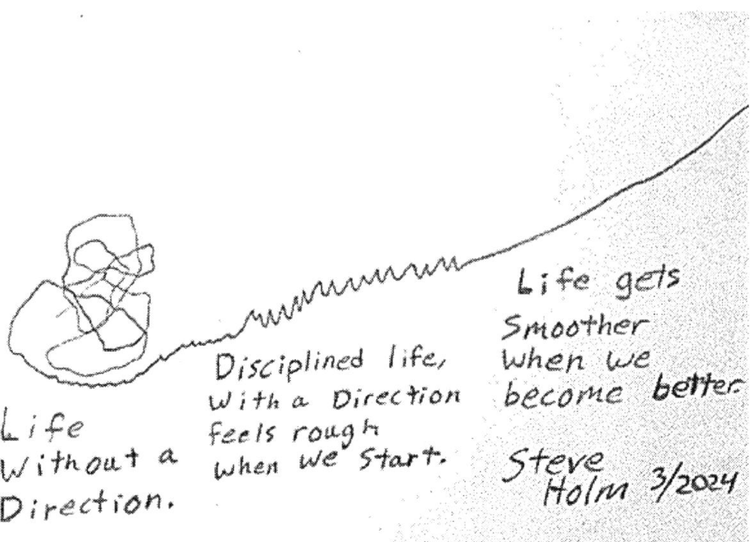

As shown in this illustration, life without a clear goal is a directionless mess. Though we might take action, the things that we do may not actually be getting us anywhere. It's only after creating goals and setting ourselves on a disciplined path (see Chapter 11) that we can escape the confusion and anxiety of aimlessness. On the disciplined path, we may experience many ups and downs. However, on this course, our lives will ultimately improve. It sends us on an upwards trajectory. This is the power of well-developed goals.

As we dive into setting personal and professional goals, it's important to remember that setting goals is all about bringing focus and substance to your dreams—not *limiting* them. Don't cut yourself short. If you set your sights on a goal 10X bigger than what you actually expect, you're sure to end up with at least double what you have. It's a cliché for a reason—when you shoot for the moon, you'll end up in the stars.

Don't shy away from your dreams for the future. Don't be afraid to stand out from the crowd, and don't let the fear of mistakes along the way stop you before you've begun. If you're worried about what could go wrong, you'll waste precious time on anxiety that should be used for action. If you're worried about what others will say, you will become what they think of you instead of what you want for yourself. It takes courage and individuality to set the right course for your life.

We inhibit our goals with our fears. We choose to live for others instead of for ourselves. But we can choose to treat our dreams with respect and cultivate goals that give us the future we deserve. This is the first step if you want to become your genuine self and find happiness in a life that is truly yours.

Setting Goals

Here's my quick to-do list for developing goals:

1. Identify what you want.
2. Identify why you want it.
3. Identify how you're going to get it.

Let's start by returning to the hunger that we talked about in the introduction. Hunger is a proactive drive for self-improvement and growth. This hunger is at the core of setting goals.

To harness this hunger, we need to analyze and dissect it. What are you really hungry for? Is it financial success, or is it really just stability? Is it fame, or is it really just self-assurance? Once you get to the heart of your hunger, you can begin to verbalize your real goals to yourself.

After you've decided what you want, take time to understand why you want it. Simon Sinek's book *Start with Why: How Great Leaders Inspire Everyone to Take Action* dives into the idea of your "Why," which serves as your driving purpose, cause, or belief. Let your inner voice guide you towards a purpose-filled goal. If your goals don't have a deep, meaningful reason behind them, it'll be difficult to maintain the momentum that you need to turn them into a reality.

Another book by Simon Sinek, *The Infinite Game,* offers some guidance when it comes to developing valuable goals. When I read his book, his core lessons stuck with me. He encouraged people to find a higher purpose to drive our actions. He also highlighted the importance of patience in reaching our goals. Personal growth is an ongoing process. If you set a truly worthy goal, it will probably take more blood, sweat, and tears than you can fit into two weeks—or even two years. It will require you to be resilient, overcome setbacks, be adaptable and remain open-minded.

So, what do you want?

Is it a million dollars? A better relationship? A profitable business? A healthy body?

Think it. Analyze it. Write it down. Then, commit to the time and effort it will take to see it come true.

Assess and Re-assess

Next, we're going to talk about fleshing out your goals. Over the course of my personal studies, I've read a lot about developing goals. One critical message that I've learned is that goal-setting is an ongoing process. It requires detailed plans, assessment, and continual self-reflection.

The following list is a compilation of my studies and my personal experience with successfully making and meeting goals.

1. Set clear goals.
2. Consider your values and priorities.
3. Assess your strengths and weaknesses.

4. Break down goals into manageable steps.
5. Seek feedback and input.
6. Re-asses your goals regularly.

First things first: setting clear goals. Once we've developed an overarching goal and we understand the drive behind it, it's important to make sure that it is (1.) clear and (2.) achievable. Take time to define your goal in detail. How will you know when you've reached it? How can it be measured? Is it relevant to you and the world around you?

After you have a more developed idea of your goals, evaluate whether they align to your personal values and how they fit into the larger picture of your life. If your goal is to be a YouTuber, but security and consistency are higher on your priority list, it's possible that your initial goal may need to be revised.

Then, we must take an honest look in the metaphysical mirror. Make an inventory of your skills, abilities, and flaws. Take this as a serious exercise—self-awareness is key to growth, and you can't have self-awareness without introspection and honesty. For visual learners, it may be helpful to sit down and make a list of your personal pros and cons. As you begin to refine your goals, consider ways that you can capitalize on your strengths and minimize the effects of your weaknesses.

Step 4 is to break your goals down into manageable steps. This is the nitty gritty. It takes a lot of time, vision, and research to plan out actionable steps. This step requires you to trace your expected route all the way from your starting point to the final destination, including notable milestones and challenges along the way. We'll talk about this in greater detail in Chapter 4.

After you've developed a plan to reach your goal, look for feedback from trusted individuals. Even if you spend all day looking in the mirror, you may never see the stain on the back of your jacket. To develop a well-rounded understanding of your goals and challenges, you need to communicate with others. Find someone with good judgement, but, most importantly, find someone who understands you and your character. When I was younger, I relied on my little brother. I'd bounce idea after idea off him and ask him for feedback. Everyone has blind spots. Instead of ignoring them, use your resources to identify them.

Last, but certainly not least: reassess your goals on the regular.

Some goals take years to reach, and the milestones may change along the way. If you were driving in an unfamiliar country without a GPS, you wouldn't check the map just once. You need to make sure that you're on the right path.

Additionally, our goals themselves may shift over time. If you find your original goals slipping away, don't panic. It's not against "the rules" to shift from one goal to another. It's never too late to change direction. When you grow, your goals may grow with you. This means that goal re-assessment should be a regular habit. "Why am I doing this?" should become your favorite question. Repeat this question multiple times a day to stay conscious of your goals and your actions.

This is a process that I've used to refine my goals, but it's just the tip of the iceberg. Be sure to add goal-setting to your research list, and seek out online resources that explore the topic in greater depth.

Going after your goals is like climbing a tall, steep ladder. You climb rung after rung. But, when you get to the top, you might realize that you've had the ladder leaned up against the wrong wall this entire time.

You've put the effort in but you're still far from your final destination. You thought it was the right wall when you got started, but, as you got closer to the top, it became clear that it wasn't going to take you where you really wanted to be. Looking back, you can see that you should have realized you were going in the wrong direction—but, since you were already committed, you ignored the signs, put your head down, and kept climbing. Now, you have to climb back down, move the ladder, and start all over. It's a recipe for frustration and wasted time.

Regularly re-assessing your goals can prevent these pitfalls. It's a habit that allows you to adjust your course—and, even if you end up having to change walls completely, it allows you to start on the right wall, sooner.

Assessing your goals and strategy to adjust your approach offers you:

Clarity. Consistent reassessment makes you reflect on your past experiences and choices. It provides an opportunity to step back and gain a fresh perspective, a process that may identify behaviors and patterns that you didn't see before.

Alignment. The self-reflection that comes with consistent assessment encourages you to stick to your priorities and make decisions that align with your core values, as well as prevent yourself from making choices that don't ultimately align with your goals. Alignment in life is just like your car—if one tire is out of alignment, it will end up wearing multiple tires down, leading to an unsteady ride.

Fulfillment. Reassessing your goals and your behaviors defines what brings you real joy and satisfaction. This can refine your goals in the long-term to fulfill your priorities and get the things that ultimately matter to you most.

Empowerment. Life is about embracing your personal power to become the person you aspire to be. It's about taking risks, stepping outside of your comfort zone, and pushing your personal boundaries. Self-discovery and self-creation are how we discover our passions and pursue our dreams. When we assess our life and goals, we give ourselves permission to make conscious choices to actively create the life that we want.

A mentor of mine recommended that I video myself while speaking publicly. Then, I could go back and rewatch the video to see how I did. This is a powerful piece of advice that centers on the importance of reflection and re-assessment. In my personal life, consistent reassessment and self-reflection has allowed me to expand my perspective. I view myself as two people: how I seem from the inside, and how I might seem from the outside. I can combine my two perspectives to understand how my behaviors might come across to those around me. Then, I take feedback from others into account and assess my behaviors to make sure that they align with what I want.

Celebrate Your Progress

Take time to acknowledge and celebrate your achievements in your personal growth. Recognize the hard work and dedication that got you to where you are. Consider keeping a journal, a to-do list, or a visual tracking system that allows you to celebrate your progress. Personally, I use photos and a journal app to document my setbacks and successes. I use it to reflect on the lessons that I've learned. When I need it, I can review this content and remember my journey so far, which keeps me on track to where I'm going.

This will also help you overcome resistance. Do you remember the last time that you had a big plan that fell apart? Sometimes, all it takes is a boss saying "no." These are moments to stop and think about how you can learn from the experience. Either tune out the haters or use it to keep yourself on the path that you want to be on. Turn the fumble into fuel.

Developing Discipline

When it comes to staying on top of our goals, a common word that we hear is "motivation." Personally, I'm with Jocko Willink on this one—I think discipline beats out motivation any day. Motivation comes and goes. It's like an inspirational poster in a windstorm. A bad mood swing would be enough to take it down.

On the other hand, discipline is a characteristic that you can develop as a permanent fixture—think a steel-bolted plaque instead of a paper poster. It'll stick around and offer you support, even when things start to look rockier than you expected.

Discipline is necessary to reach your goals, because underneath the happy, golden ideals that you have for your future is a seething underbelly of hard work and sacrifice. Take the concept of a dream job—not a bad idea, on paper. A job that would bring you success and fulfillment is a good goal to have. Let's go back to that dream of being a YouTuber. It's a good job if you have a passion for sharing what you do, and you like the passive income model that comes from longform videos.

However, even this job has its drawbacks. You'll find that the average successful YouTuber pours hours of energy into writing scripts, editing videos, and making sponsor deals. Maybe they're losing sleep from the pressure of maintaining a schedule. They're often sweating over strategies to beat the algorithm so they can make rent that month.

This isn't to say that you shouldn't go after your dream job—but it won't be a fulfilled dream if you don't go into it with an understanding that achieving your goals takes a mountain of effort.

Discipline is about learning what is good for you, not what is easy. To change your life, you have to change your life's patterns. Humans tend to fight change and cling to comfort. You have to be willing to sacrifice comfort and stick to the grind. You have to train your mind to love change and to face challenges head-on. It's a necessity if you want to develop the discipline that you need to chase your goals, even in the face of resistance and obstacles.

When you find yourself knee-deep in the muddy terrain, consider your predecessors. Remember the people from previous generations that created the opportunities that you have today. How many hundreds and thousands of hours went into inventing the lightbulb? How many hours are you going to put in to changing your life—or even improving the world?

Realizing Your Goals

Adam Grant's book *Hidden Potential* features three major steps to unlocking your full capacity. According to Adam, we first have to recognize and leverage our unique strengths. Then, we have to embrace experimentation and be willing to explore new things and step out of our comfort zone. Finally, we have to make a commitment to personal development and maintain a growth mindset so that we're devoted to reaching our full potential. This allows us to start recognizing our talents and tie them to our goals. However, if we rely too much on the talents that we have, we end up boxing ourselves into our comfort zone. Your goals can rarely be achieved by staying in your comfort zone. If they can, you may be limiting your goals based on your fears of performance. If you want to live a better life, you have to be willing to leave the life that you have. *Hidden Potential* teaches us that we have to be committed to continual improvement. Once we reach our goals, that doesn't mean that we're ready to sit down and die. There should always be another thing that we're looking for, another change that we want to make in our lives, or at least another item to cross off our bucket list.

Deciding that you are done after you reach your initial goal is cutting yourself off from endless opportunities that could await you ahead. That's why we can't just obsess over the goal itself, we have to become addicted to progress if we want to maintain forward motion and continually improve.

My overall goal is to be the best version of myself. No one is on the same path that I am on. I am able to work every day to be better than the day before. Embrace the journey of self-discovery and self-fulfillment. Live a life that is always focused forward.

References for Future Learning

Hidden Potential: The Science of Achieving Greater Things by Adam Grant

Start with Why: How Great Leaders Inspire Everyone to Take Action by Simon Sinek

Success Through a Positive Mental Attitude by Napoleon Hill and W. Clement Stone

The Compound Effect by Darren Hardy

The Infinite Game by Simon Sinek

CHAPTER 4

Building Strategic Vision

"Don't get wrapped around tactical competition. Think strategic all the time."

—Jocko Willink

For most of the 20th century, Kodak was one of the world's largest manufacturers for film and cameras. It was a pioneer for making photography accessible to the masses. In the first two decades of its life, Kodak rapidly expanded to the European market and, through a series of continual innovations, dominated the photography and film market for decades.

Kodak's research labs invented the first digital camera in 1975. A decade later, they also invented the first megapixel digital camera, which made independent digital photography a conceivable reality.

Yet, in spite of its own inventions, the leaders at Kodak believed that digital photography posed a threat to their business model, which relied at the time on individuals using their services to print photos. Resisting the digital revolution, the Kodak company clung to their success with traditional film.

In 2012, Kodak filed for bankruptcy, and it has since failed to regain a significant foothold in the industry.

Kodak suffered from a collapse in strategic vision. Strategic vision is all about conceptualizing how you, your organization, or your business will plan for the future. It connects data to formulate plans that align with your primary goals. It's the driving force for innovative ideas. Before its resistance to digital photography, Kodak had been on the cutting edge of the industry. If it had stayed with its strategic vision as an industry leader rather than trying to remain comfortable and address its immediate fiscal concerns, Kodak might still be the leading brand in photography and film.

We can look back on our lives right now and pinpoint decisions that we've made that have either helped us reach success or prevented it. A few years from now, you'll be looking back on the decisions you're making today. The strategy that you develop in the present can either get you closer to your ideal future or take you further away from it. If goals are our final destination, our strategic vision is our overarching game plan for how we're going to get there.

So, how do we build a strategic vision for our future?

In his book *Elevate: The Three Disciplines of Advanced Strategic Thinking,* Rich Horwath defines three disciplines to develop strategic skills. While these disciplines were originally written as advice for business strategy, they apply to strategic thinking in every area of our lives.

1. Coalesce. As Kenichi Ohmae, legendary business theorist and strategist, said, "Analysis is the critical starting point of strategic thinking." This step requires us to analyze different insights to develop our strategies. To figure out the right steps for us, we first have to have an understanding of where we are, where we want to go, and the challenges that we may face on the way. This is also where we look back on our past successes through an analytical lens. What led to our past accomplishments? Take time to identify positive and negative patterns in your life that can be applied to your strategy.

2. Compete. Creating a system of strategies shouldn't just be about surviving. Our strategic vision should lead us to have a competitive advantage.

3. Champion. In life and business, we do not succeed or fail on our own. We should develop a strategy to lead and inspire others to work with us and inform our overall vision.

We can use Rich Horwath's guide to develop a strategic vision for every area of our lives, whether we're trying to build our credit over the next year or plan for the financial security of our family.

Strategic Planning

Strategic vision informs strategic planning. Consider what you've learned in the first chapters of this book. Our mindset informs our strategic vision, and our perspective informs our strategic planning to execute our vision. It's about developing an idea and working to execute it in the best possible way.

Strategic planning is what enables organizations and individuals to set clear goals and objectives. It's vital to define the steps that will allow you to achieve your overall goals and allocate your resources and time effectively. Planning provides direction and focus, helps us coordinate between different involved parties, and allows us to reduce risk and wasted energy. Plus, when we plan our futures strategically, we're able to adapt in rapidly changing environments. Winners in life and in business plan strategically to inform their current decisions so that they can reap future rewards.

In our personal lives, strategic planning is necessary to reach the goals that we want. It's about living life intentionally. It may seem silly to plan out personal milestones that you'd like to reach in your development, but it gives you a valuable outline for reaching fulfillment. If you want success in your personal growth, there's no better way to get started than to make a concrete plan. Houses don't buy themselves, and families don't build themselves; even in your personal life, a strategic plan is a major asset.

In *Think and Grow Rich,* author Napoleon Hill gives guidelines for developing strategies that are beneficial for strategic planning in our personal lives. His primary guidelines start with visualizing your success and developing a deep desire to realize your goals. Then, he encourages us to take decisive action, surround ourselves with people who support our vision, and continuously seek opportunities for learning and improvement so that we can achieve long-term success.

In the world of business, a good strategic plan can be the difference between a successful project and a failed one. This is particularly true if you want to own your own business. Patrick Bet-David's book *Your Next Five Moves: Master the Art of Business Strategy* describes the five steps towards strategic planning for developing your business.

Step 1. Understand yourself.
Step 2. Solve problems effectively.
Step 3. Build a winning team.
Step 4. Strategize to scale up.
Step 5. Get good at powerplays.

This is a more detailed guide that resembles Rich Horwath's 3 guidelines in *Elevate: The Three Disciplines of Advanced Strategic Thinking*. Patrick Bet-David teaches us that we must begin by understanding ourselves and our vision for a business, then strategize for potential obstacles, brainstorm ways to expand, and develop strategies for maintaining the business in the long-term. Alongside these guides, I urge you to seek out business experts on YouTube.

They often share the most up-to-date information on business strategy.

Strategize to Avoid Setbacks

It's true that some challenges are unavoidable. It's one of the reasons that you need to plan on hard work to achieve your goals. However, thinking strategically lets you dodge unnecessary setbacks—particularly those that are self-inflicted.

One of the greatest lessons that strategic vision gives you is sacrificing short-term pain for long-term gain. Consider those who smoke. When you intake nicotine, your body responds by releasing dopamine. The short term high from smoking is tempting enough that millions in the United States alone have developed a nicotine habit.

The picture in the long-term is starkly different. Organ damage, lung cancer, and brain impairment are all likely to creep in. It gets worse—smoking also deals significant damage to your mental health. Those who smoke are literally choosing a superficial short-term happiness now over real, long-term happiness later.

Even if you don't personally smoke, chances are that you've given in to short-term happiness over long-term fulfillment before. This is a setback that quality strategic thinking can save you from.

To live strategically, practice thinking for both the immediate and distant future. Think about how your decisions will affect you five days from now. Consider the immediate consequences, the drawbacks, the effort. Then, think about how those actions could influence you five years from now. Difficult decisions now often lead to easy decisions in the future. Current sacrifice leads to future success. If you live with this five-day and five-year picture in your mind, you'll be driven to make better decisions that benefit you in the long term, even if they require short-term sacrifice.

When I was trying to build my credit, I knew I had to implement strategic thinking to achieve my goals. I started by researching credit card companies, reading up on the merits of the company and what type of credits they offer. After I chose the right company for me, I got a personal loan, which I gradually paid back with my own money. I didn't have to get the loan. In fact, the interest meant that I spent more money than if I hadn't taken up the loan. However, it did build my credit. It was short term pain for long term gain.

This kind of strategic sacrifice is necessary for creating a plan that will lead to your ultimate goals. Account for things that you may have to give up. Trust me—your goals are worth it. Begin developing a defined strategy with measurable benchmarks, and you'll catapult yourself on the right path to get what you truly want.

References for Future Learning

Become a Great Strategic Thinker | Ian Bremmer," from YouTube channel *Big Think*

Elevate: The Three Disciplines of Advanced Strategic Thinking by Rich Horwath

"How to Think Strategically as a Leader," from YouTube channel *David Burkus*

"Simon Sinek on How to Improve Strategic Thinking," from YouTube channel *Capture Your Flag*

"Strategic: The Skill to Set Direction, Create Advantages, and Achieve Executive Excellence," from YouTube channel *Rich Horwath*

Think and Grow Rich by Napoleon Hill

Your Next Five Moves: Master the Art of Business Strategy by Patrick Bet-David

CHAPTER 5

Finding Your Focus

"Success without fulfillment is the ultimate failure."

—Tony Robbins

Take a minute to brainstorm your purpose in life and in your career. For this exercise, let's stay centered on your end goal, rather than your next milestone. Try to clearly describe your end goal in one sentence. Keep it short and snappy—make it something you could explain in ten seconds. This will force you to find get right to the heart the matter.

This should be your focus.

No need to complicate things. Focus is just what it says on the tin. Your focus is what you pay attention to. When your focus is on your life goals, it means that they are a priority in your life. That's where you commit your time, energy, and thoughts. It's possible for you to have a well-defined goal and detailed strategy without committing it to your focus. Without this focus, life becomes like driving while texting. Your attention is divided, so you're more likely to crash, swerve, and miss your exit.

As we discussed in chapters 1 and 2, the things that we focus on determine who we are. In Chapter 4, we talked about how those who are driven focus on lasting joy, and others focus on short-term pleasure. From this, we learn that you end up going after whatever you keep your mind on. Focusing on your purpose needs to be your number one priority if you're planning on making progress. Laser focus is the best way to follow your strategized plan and achieve your goals. When you have the sense of purpose that comes from focusing on the right elements of your life, you avoid wasting time and effort on unimportant roadblocks. This enables you to work with greater direction towards personal and professional fulfillment.

On the other hand, if you're focused on your past mistakes, you won't be able to live for the present. If you're focused on others' problems, you'll miss the chance to fix your own. If you're focused on trivial challenges in your life, you'll fail to appreciate your opportunities.

Avoiding Distraction

So, where is your focus? Is it on your work, your relationships? Are you focused on your life's mission? Your personal goals?

For many of us, we don't even know where our focus is—or how it ended up there.

Today, there are hundreds of different things vying for our attention. We have to wade through distractions from every side. Work responsibilities can distract us from our families. Family responsibilities can distract us from our self-growth journeys. And, with remarkable force, the present world can distract us from our personal futures.

The current state of technology means that most of us are constantly available to the world at large. Social media calls for our attention at all hours of the day. News alerts notify us about events taking place all around the globe. Our phones are instant connections to every person in our lives.

As advice, I'm going to tell you something that you've heard before: turn off your phone.

I was once speaking to a rich friend of mine who always left his phone on silent mode, and often didn't take it with him. I watched this habit for days, and then I finally asked, "Why don't you seem to care about your phone calls?"

He answered, "I pretty much control my space. I'll gladly call someone back when I get around to picking my phone up again, but I'm not going to hand my life over to whoever wants to call me and let them dictate my schedule. When it works for me, I'll call them back and we can have a conversation."

This is one of the great ways that you can help yourself. You are not a 24-hour diner. You have not committed to always being available. The world can give you ten minutes or two hours.

Commit a few hours of every day to "focus time." Set your phone to do not disturb mode. Put a sign up on your office door: "Focusing for the next hour. Please email me, and I'll follow up with you." Setting these boundaries establishes your control over your time and space—which can improve your focus and motivation. Jocko Willink, a podcaster and author that we'll see more of in this book, swears by this method of avoiding distraction. When he was in school, Jocko would sit down and tell himself, "I'm not leaving this room until I've read a full chapter." If these techniques just aren't cutting it, don't give up. The internet's not just full of distraction. There's an endless stream of free advice online for improving your focus. Seek out new methods and find what works for you.

Tell yourself that it's your focus time. Then, set the phone down. Read the chapter. Study for the exam. Make the plans that will bring you closer to your dreams.

Keeping this focus time allows you to give others the adequate attention that they need. If they're trying to address a serious concern with you, you want to be able to focus on them entirely—not being half-concerned with the to-do list that you were in the middle of completing.

We have the fastest connection of any previous generation. If your grandpa could wait a week to get a letter, you can wait one hour to read a text. But what if something urgent happens, and someone *needs* to get in touch with you? Try developing alternative ways for others to reach out in case of emergency, such as calling the main office instead of your personal phone or adjusting your settings on your cell so that certain contacts still come through with notifications.

This method is a great way to approach your life and relationships with discipline and respect. Just be sure to communicate with the people in your life so that they understand that this is a new habit that you're working on. The extra time can help you maintain the right level of focus for both your responsibilities and your relationships with others.

Focus on What You Control

Let's say you're waiting for your flight at the airport. Shortly before your plane is supposed to arrive, you hear an announcement that your flight has been delayed.

Now, you have a decision to make. You can groan and complain. You can yell at the airport employee like they are personally responsible for the delay. You can tie yourself into frustrated knots and spend the added wait time fuming in your seat.

None of these actions will make your plane arrive on time.

Luckily, you have another option. You can acknowledge that you can't personally pull the plane across the sky. Then, you can find a good book to read, take a moment to meditate, or use the time to finish up extra odds and ends.

You could choose to focus on external forces beyond your control, or you could focus on what you can control. Down one option, you get easily irritated, upset, and frustrated. Down the other, you're able to remain calm and even get some work done. The temptation towards the first option is strong. When we entrench ourselves in what we can't control, it excuses our lack of action. It allows us to place responsibility for our circumstances on the people around us, instead of on ourselves.

When we focus on what we can control, we take responsibility for our own life and circumstances. This empowers us to make real change. This same logic applies to every situation in our life, whether we're facing relationship problems or workplace miscommunications.

A friend of mine got a speeding ticket and came to me for advice. He was wondering if he should fight it in court or if he should just pay the fine. When he was ticketed, he had definitely been speeding, but he hoped to talk the judge into lowering his penalty. It was a habit he didn't want to break, because, as he said, "Driving slower than the speed limit is boring."

He can't control what the judge decides, and he can't control the policeman watching for speeders on the shoulder of the highway. However, he can control what he does to solve his problem in the future.

I told him that he needed to find something else to engage his mind while driving. He needed to find a good audiobook to listen to on his daily commute. This would keep him engaged during the drive. Plus, it might be interesting enough that he might not even be in a rush to save those few extra minutes on his commute.

In this way, focusing on what we can control enables us to analyze and solve problems. It's the first step to being solution-oriented as a habit.

Becoming Solution-Oriented

Being solution-oriented means that you don't waste time hyper-analyzing, bemoaning, and complaining about the problem—whatever the problem may be. Whether it's a delayed flight or a missed promotion, people who are solution-oriented take it on the chin and find the best way to move forward.

There's a viral YouTube video by director Jason Headley called "It's Not About the Nail." It's a perfect illustration of how some people approach problems. The video opens with a woman explaining that she has a painful headache, and she doesn't know what's causing it. Then, the camera zooms out to show that she has a nail driven into her forehead. She complains about her incessant headaches, her insomnia, and her snagged sweaters. She says, "There's all this pressure, you know, and sometimes it feels like it's right up on me, and I can just feel it, literally feel it, in my head." Her husband answers, "Well, you do have a nail in your head." Her reply?

"It is *not* about the nail."

This is the trap that we fall into when we refuse to be solution-oriented. In this instance, the woman is so focused on the effects of the problem that she refuses to see the root of them. This is what it means to be obsessed with your problems. If she was solution-oriented, she would have been openly looking for solutions, even if it required painful change—like removing the nail.

Remaining focused on what we can control is one of the greatest secrets to overcoming challenges and becoming solution-oriented, even in the face of tremendous difficulty.

Ever heard the saying, "It never rains, but it pours"? Often, life doesn't wait for one problem to go away before giving you another. Life is famous for giving out plural lemon*s,* not just one.

In these circumstances, focus is more important than ever. On Jocko Willink's official *Jocko Podcast,* a listener came looking for advice. She was facing financial and personal problems that kept adding up. How was she supposed to dig herself out when her challenges seemed to be compounding?

Jocko answered, "Prioritize and execute. What's the biggest problem? What's causing the most stress?"

Simple enough advice, but it can be a lifeline when you're navigating stressful situations. If you're drowning, focus on finding flat ground before worrying about your wet clothes. When you approach the biggest problems with a solution-oriented perspective, you can develop actionable plans that get you out of the water.

As for execute? Jocko makes it clear that it's not just about being solution-oriented—you've got to be willing to put the work in. He continued, "These challenges that you face, they're going to do their best to take you down. Do not let them. Stand up. Dig in. Line up those problems and confront them. Face them. Fight them." Become solution-oriented—and then be prepared to solve.

One day, I was dealing with a lot of compound challenges in my life. I was low, depressed, and getting sick of the grind. I was suffering from such severe brain fog that I wasn't even able to think clearly. After spending a frustrating amount of time trying to get my mind to run normally, I finally realized that I was focusing on the wrong problem. I immediately researched ways to overcome my brain fog. I found acupressure points. I drank water, ate some blueberries, and did a lot of praying and deep breathing.

Through these changes, I overcame my first, most basic problem, which added clarity and precision to my thoughts. From there, I was better equipped to handle the challenges that life was throwing at me. Focus on what you can control, and then focus on the right problems.

Focus, Responsibility, and Relationships

It's all good and fine to focus on what we can control in actionable situations—but what about interpersonal relationships? If your spouse won't put their clothes in the hamper, how is it your fault? If your friend expects you to do everything in the relationship, how are you supposed to encourage *them* to take responsibility?

It's a delicate balance. Focusing on what you can control doesn't mean taking control of every situation—and it doesn't mean ignoring the things that you can't control. Just like keeping a positive mindset doesn't mean ignoring all of the negativity, focusing on yourself doesn't mean that you're not affected by other people. Particularly in personal relationships, allowing "uncontrollable" issues to go unsaid in an effort to focus on what you can control will ultimately contribute to a breakdown of communication and trust.

While you can't control what the people around you do, you can control how you address the issue. Whether they're aware of the problem or not, be sure to approach them with a positive attitude and a grateful heart. In any relationship, whether you are spouses, friends, or parent and child, keep in mind that the other person does not want to upset you. They actively want what is best for your relationship. This is true even if there are some difficulties that you have to overcome to get there. It's important to make this shift in your mind, as it will take you off the defense and inspire you to work towards solutions instead of hurt feelings.

Think of it like this; when you have difficulties in your relationships, it's like a brick wall is separating you from the other person. You don't know what they're doing on their side. Sometimes, you might think that they're adding bricks maliciously to frustrate you. You can yell, scream, fight, kick—but being angry will not take down the wall. The only way to bring the wall down is for both parties to work together.

Here's some of my best advice that you can take upon yourself when it comes to working out problems with others. By following this advice, you can work closer to resolution while keeping the focus on what you can control.

Choose the right time. If you have something serious to talk about, make sure it's in a private setting during a time where neither you nor the other person are stressed or overwhelmed. This can ensure that you're both in the right mindset to communicate.

Listen actively. Allow them to express their perspective. Don't listen to respond—a habit where you're more focused on constructing your rebuttal than listening to what they're saying. Instead, listen to understand.

Collaborate. Instead of criticism, direct the conversation in the direction of collaboration. It's the both of you against the problem, not against each other. Ask the person what they recommend.

Use "I" statements. This small shift allows you to shoulder your responsibility in every situation. Consider the difference between these two sentences:

"You're always leaving laundry on the floor!"

"I feel frustrated when I see laundry on the floor."

This avoids placing blame on others and clearly defines your perspective. In response, the other person can share their perspective.

These steps prompt you to take responsibility for your own actions and evaluate your own behaviors. This self-awareness ultimately leads to personal growth and strengthens relationships in the long term. Keep in mind that interpersonal communication is one of the most challenging skills to master. Consider these as brief guidelines, and be sure to flesh out your understanding by seeking out more information, particularly through online resources.

Approach with empathy, a willingness to communicate, and a focus on your personal actions, and you can work through interpersonal problems at every level. Dr. Kevin Leman's parenting book *Have a New Teenager by Friday,* a guide on communicating effectively, setting boundaries, and building a healthy relationship with teens. This book explains a teenagers' emotional and physical needs as they work towards adult responsibilities and independence, but its main message isn't about changing the teens—it's about how parents can create a respectful home environment to navigate this stage of parenthood more effectively. In interpersonal relationships, there will always be someone else to blame. The only way to break the cycle is to focus on yourself and what you can control.

References for Future Learning

Delivering Happiness by Tony Hsieh

Have a New Teenager by Friday by Dr. Kevin Leman

Origin USA, a YouTube channel by Jocko Willink

CHAPTER 6

Money

"If you want to be rich, do what rich people do."

—Dave Ramsey

One day, I got out my calculator and started computing how much work I would have to do to make a million dollars. I took my hourly wage and multiplied it by my weekly work time. I tried to figure out how many weeks it would take before I'd earned a million dollars total, not counting expenses. Eventually, I stared at my income on the calculator, and I thought, "How can I add three zeroes to that number?"

For the next two chapters, we're going to talk about an all-important topic that finds its way into most of the self-growth literature out there: money. Financial advisors, life coaches, and self-help gurus alike are all eager to share their advice on how to get, keep, and grow your funds. It's nearly universal. But if self-growth is all about internal improvement rather than external validation, why do we care about money so much?

Whether we like it or not, money plays a big role in our daily lives. Money struggles can increase our stress, affect our relationships, and even impact our health. We have to manage our money correctly if we want to overcome these challenges. Money is essential to stability, longevity, and innovation. If we seek excellence in our lives, we have to seek excellence in our finances.

In the right hands, money becomes a valuable tool for improving yourself and the world around you. More than a liability that you have to manage, money is an opportunity to enact significant change.

To provide a well-rounded perspective on this important subject, I've divided it into two chapters. This chapter focuses on the way that we think about money. In the next chapter, we'll dive into specific financial concepts, such as debt, taxes, and cash flow. But for now, let's talk about setting monetary goals, finding financial role models, and changing the way that we understand wealth so that we can make our money work for us.

Monetary Goals

In *Seven Habits of Highly Effective People*, author and educator Steven Covey emphasizes the importance of beginning with the end in mind. As with any goal (see Chapter 3), your financial journey must start with a vision of what you want and an understanding of where you are.

As you start to envision your financial future, you'll probably hear a nagging question in the back of your head: how much money can you *really* get?

My answer: however much you really want.

The story at the beginning of this chapter was inspired by Tony Robbins's *Money Master: The Game.* In this book, Tony provides detailed instructions for doing the math to see what you need to do to achieve your financial goals. These kinds of exercises teach us that our financial goals aren't really that improbable—so long as we're willing to outwork and outthink others for it.

Using the strategies that we've discussed in chapters 3 and 4, brainstorm what you want in your financial future. Your financial goal could be the investments that you want to have, the level of income, or just a flat dollar amount. Like your life goals, financial goals should be in both the short- and long-term. Consider if you want to save for a down payment on a mortgage, pay off a debt, or build your retirement fund. These clear goals give you something to work towards to prioritize your spending and saving habits.

Once you've prepared your financial end goals, you're ready to begin making the necessary changes to reach those goals. The biggest first step that you can take in the right direction is finding financial role models.

You wouldn't go to a pro-basketball player to learn how to perform surgery. Don't go to an average person to learn how to live exceptionally. There are people out there that have already gotten exactly what you want. You just need to find out how they did it.

Learning from role models is an ideal way to build your finances. The economy is influenced by so many countless factors that keeping up-to-date with the strategies of your icons can be more valuable than sticking with tried-and-true tactics.

Luckily, it's easier to learn from financial experts than ever before. Many of the most successful people in the financial sector openly share their most important advice in the form of films, books, and podcasts—and many even offer advice for free online in YouTube videos and blogs. These are useful guides if you want to follow in their footsteps and match their financial moves.

As you research, you'll find that different individuals have radically different approaches. This allows you to consider the pros and cons of each approach and find the right method for you. Grant Cardone, Robert Kiyosaki, and Kris Krohn are all great examples of highly successful individuals that worked up to their ideal lifestyle in their own unique ways. For example, some of these role models use debt to leverage investments, while others inform you on ways to avoid debt to reach your goals. Take advantage of all of these examples. They allow you to more fully understand the many layers that go into financial success.

Be sure to check out the resources for future learning that are included throughout this book, and particularly at the end of this chapter. When it comes to setting and realizing your financial goals, a concrete example can make all of the difference.

Allow yourself to be picky. You should only listen to those who resonate with your financial vision. For instance, Dave Ramsey is a highly successful financial coach, but I don't personally follow his overarching financial plan. Dave Ramsey is a name that you've probably heard before—we've even already mentioned him in this book. While some of his ideas resonate with me, I feel that his advice is meant for someone looking for average financial success. Since I want my financial goals to take me farther, I've turned my attention to other financial role models for advice and guidance.

Alongside financial role models, it's a good idea to surround yourself with others who share your goals. Seek out mentors or join communities filled with like-minded individuals. When you surround yourself with positive and motivated people, you can encourage each other to meet your financial goals and share advice and information.

Don't underestimate the power of your social feed. Follow and subscribe to people who share your financial goals or are living them as a reality. Get on every social media platform you have and hunt down the top three people who inspire you financially. Then, the next time you pick up your phone and start scrolling, at least a part of your feed will be offering you financial guidance. Extra inspiration, no effort.

If you want to be a millionaire, you must do what the millionaires do. If you want to up that to a billionaire, you need to study the habits and life stories of the billionaires. If you want to be broke, keep asking all of your broke friends for money advice. They'll do the best they can for you.

The Abundance Mindset

Remember: inflation is killing the dollar. Your options are limited. The world is against you. There's absolutely no way you can build exponential wealth.

For many of us, these common mantras ring in our head every day. They're getting in our way.

As you begin this leg of your financial growth, take time to analyze your current beliefs about money. Over time, many of us develop negative attitudes that hold us back from realizing our financial futures.

Begin breaking down these thoughts. Sift out what is true from what has merely been taught to you. You'll find that exponential wealth is never out of reach—and that the only one who can truly limit your options is you.

Try restructuring these negative concepts about money so that they leave room for growth. Instead of thinking, "Money is for the rich," try, "Money is for the rich, so I need to start learning the game that the rich play." Rather than worrying that there isn't enough money in the world for little old you to reach your financial goals, start developing the abundance mindset.

The abundance mindset is the opposite of the poverty mindset. Poverty tells us that our funds are getting low. Abundance tells us that our dwindling bank account isn't the only place to find money. This mindset keeps us from counting pennies and instead focuses us on accumulating future wealth and long-term security. I'll repeat a favorite quote of Robert Kiyosaki's: "Instead of telling yourself that you cannot afford something, start asking yourself how you can afford it."

In 2023, there is enough money for every human on planet Earth to have a net worth of $625,000. If we narrow this down to just the United States, that means the citizens of this country would be worth $14,749,262.50. That's $14,749,262.50 of potential. If we laid each of those dollar bills end-to-end, it would travel around the earth 2,725 times before we'd run out of money. That's more than 2/3 of the way to the sun.

Feel free to check my numbers on this, but no matter how you slice it, there's plenty of money in the world. You just need to get your fair share of it.

I think we sometimes do ourselves a disservice. Because of our finances, we choose to limit our lives. Instead, we should expand our finances to fit our lives in them. I have personally had my fair share of financial hard times. I remember a time when money was tight, and I realized I would need to cancel certain things that I prioritized in my life. I might have to cut coffee, cancel gym memberships, and stop my vitamin subscriptions. These were things I used to maintain my health and fitness.

I decided that these expenses were important to me. I stopped looking for ways to cut back on my spending. Instead, I chose to go out and use every available avenue to make more money.

If you nixed your daily $7 coffee, it would only save you $250 a month. That means, instead of cutting coffee, you just need a plan to make $250 more per month. It could come down to cutting back on a few coffees for a time, but planning on ways to meet your financial needs is a better long-term solution than trying to eliminate them.

Anyone who's been through hard times knows that $250 a month isn't a small thing. It's not to say that the price tag should just roll off your shoulders. But, when you commit to getting what you want as a long-term solution, with an abundance mindset in place, you're far more likely to find a way. It could be a matter of months or years before you reach that financial threshold. Chances are, it will take a lot of consistent effort and intentional action. But if you want to keep certain behaviors and expenses on your list of financial possibilities, never talk yourself into believing that you can't make it happen.

At this moment, there are rich people in the world who were once where you are now. It doesn't matter how much money you currently have in your bank account. I can almost guarantee you that someone out there has reached your financial goals starting from your current dollar amount. What you want to achieve is 100% possible. If you don't do it, someone else will. Trust me, you don't want to look around ten years down the line and wonder how someone else achieved your dreams.

To the young teenage reader—you may feel limited by your circumstances. It can be hard to get going on your financial goals as a minor. But you don't have to wait to work towards your goals. It all starts in your brain. Whether you're thirteen or thirty, now is the time to invest in your personal education. Read 50 good books before you turn 18. Find YouTubers and podcasters that share your dreams. Constantly seek out online resources. This will take you miles ahead of professionals with years of experience in your chosen field.

Let's say you have a dream of starting a small business, but you're too young to operate on a large scale. The teenager who develops a commitment to starting early would consider mowing the lawn or raking leaves for their neighbors. These are only a few ideas to get you started—with a little bit of online research, you're sure to find even more relevant opportunities. You're never too young to develop the right financial mindset and begin elevating your life. No matter your circumstances, you must focus on creating an abundance mindset if you want to reach success.

Work Smarter, Not Harder

Being a hard worker is never a bad thing. The genuine effort that you put into your work will be reflected in the quality of what you produce. However, to reach financial security, you don't just have to work harder—you also have to work smarter. The more thought you put into your actions, the easier it will be for you to make money; the easier it is, the more money you can make.

Richard Koch, venture capital investor and author, proposes a new way to think about our income: the 80/20 principle. He shows us that 80% of our results often come from 20% of our efforts. On the flip side, 80% of our efforts are wasted on only 20% of our results. If we take time to analyze our work, we can identify the high-leverage activities that yield the most significant outcomes in our lives. By simply doing more of these highly-effective activities, we can get more than 100% of our usual results. This encourages us to prioritize our behaviors, remove bottle necks, delegate responsibly, and outsource to the right people.

Grant Cardone's book *The Millionaire Booklet: How to Get Super Rich* outlines the right mindset that we need to adopt to attain financial success. With expert insights into the world of money and financial management, *The Millionaire Booklet* is a valuable roadmap for those looking to meet their financial goals. Cardone asks the simplest but most profound question at the heart of getting money:

Who has the money you want?

If you can answer that question, your financial planning will be ten times easier. Instead of wandering from avenue to avenue to find the best source of income, you can work the system backwards. These are the people who I want to pay me. What do *they* want? How can I convince them to choose me over alternative options?

This process was at the heart of why I decided to get into real estate. I found that the majority of Americans spend most of their money on housing. It was a service that allowed me to supply a place to call home in exchange for a steady income. My audience is the average American, so my residential real estate tactics are aimed towards them.

From there, it's just a matter of putting in the leg work to get their money into your pockets—or finding the right person to do the work for you.

That's where delegation comes in as a vital skill. Dan Sullivan and Benjamin Hardy's book *Who Not How* tells us that we need to focus on who to hire to perform tasks instead of figuring out how to perform tasks. This book gives us great advice for finding the right people, leveraging the talents of those around us, and investing in long-term business and financial relationships. It offers practical strategies for identifying and collaborating with others to drive personal and professional growth.

Who Not How authors Dan Sullivan and Benjamin Hardy tell the story of a rich man who tried to save some money on his new air conditioner by replacing it himself instead of hiring it out. While he was replacing the unit, he slipped, fell, and nearly died. Alongside all of the financial and emotional burden that comes from medical emergencies, this one event also cost him years in recovery.

Remember—this man wasn't on a tight budget. He could have paid $7,000 for someone else to update his AC. In the end, his DIY installment ended up costing him well over the initial amount in medical expenses alone. He was tripping over dollars to save pennies.

This is an extreme example of what we do in our daily lives. It's a product of the poverty mindset. We devalue our time in the face of our (perceived) lack of money.

When you start harnessing the skills we've discussed in this book, you make your time productive and important. Wasted time isn't just a few hours down the drain—it's a plan that won't be realized, a good idea that won't be discovered, and progress that won't be made. Sometimes, to afford the things that we want, we have to hire them out.

In this book, we've talked about focusing on yourself and maximizing your personal strength. With that in mind, delegating can feel like sapping off of others. In reality, delegation is a valuable tool. You should focus on what you can do—and, occasionally, what you can do is rely on the right people to reach your goals. Effective delegation requires us to find the right people for the right things and build mutually beneficial relationships. If you oversaw the marketing for a new company, you'd find the best graphic designer to make your logo, the best web developer to build your website, and the best artists to create your visuals. They benefit from working with you, and, instead of using your time to learn graphic design and coding, you can focus on your marketing strategy to make the company a financial success. This is how we make other people pay our bills.

Financial Wisdom

Here are some statistics for you: I have friends who work 2X as much as I do, yet earn half of my income. So far, I've read 125 more books than they have. Financial education matters—both for developing your financial fluency and keeping you up to date on the latest trends.

Financial wisdom is a bone-deep understanding of how money works. It requires us to be aware of current market trends and economic conditions to make well-informed investment decisions. Continuous education is the only way to stay up on financial news, strategies, and expert advice. If I gave you the hard-and-fast steps for the best way to make money at the time I'm writing this, by the time this book got published, it would be old news. The world changes too fast not to regularly check in on the taglines.

Financial wisdom breeds expertise, which leads to positive experiences. H. Brown Jackson Jr.'s book *Live and Learn and Pass It On* includes a quote that's particularly relevant to financial wisdom. It says, "I've learned that when a man with money meets a man with experience, the man with experience ends up with the money and the man with the money ends up with experience." Continuous financial education allow us to avoid the unnecessary risks and unexpected pitfalls that come with money management. New information can inform instant, major change. You won't be able to open new doors with old keys. Our tactics have to change, and that means that we have to keep learning long after we get out of school.

Don't get stuck in the average group by learning what average people learn. Read books, listen to podcasts, and seek out financial advisors and mentors. This growing knowledge base enables you to make informed decisions, develop a healthier relationship with money, and, eventually, achieve financial wisdom. No matter what industry you want to go into, chances are that you can find literature that gives you tangible advice for success. Books like Gary Keller's *The Million Dollar Real Estate Agent* guided me on my personal financial journey by providing foundational principles that would increase my cash flow while streamlining my business and similar investments.

Don't limit yourself to what you read in books—yep, even this book. Be sure to take full advantage of your resources by intentionally falling down financial internet rabbit holes. All of your research will accumulate to inform your financial decisions.

Continual learning is one of the greatest strategies for financial success that I can give you, and that means that you have to develop an important character trait. It's something financial winners have, and that losers are forced to learn: humility. Winners never believe that they know everything they need to know. They're aways looking to know more to refine their habits and financial decisions.

Money Takes Change

While this financial knowledge is foundational to your long-term growth, it's not enough on its own. I'll stick my neck out to disagree with the well-known adage. Knowledge *isn't* power. It's potential power. Knowledge requires action before it can become power.

Dave Ramsey, finance mogul and coach, says, "Live like no one else, so that later you can live like no one else." We must be willing to make sacrifices now if we want to live an above-average life later. The man that makes it to the top of the mountain didn't fall up there. The best views are only reached by the most challenging hikes. Everything takes work, and our finances are no different. Reaching our financial goals takes true, bone-deep commitment. There's no room for that maybe-I'll-do-it-later attitude at the millionaire's table.

Yet neglecting our financial health is an easy pit to fall into. For many people, finances are a big source of stress. And so, we do what we do best with stress: we ignore it. Talking about money is impolite. Finances are a taboo at the dinner table. In the rare opportunities that we do take to talk about it, we complain. We don't have enough in savings. Our jobs don't pay us enough. Everything is so expensive, nowadays.

Unfortunately, even if we ignore money, money does not ignore us. The main idea in Darren Hardy's book *The Compound Effect* is that compound interest doesn't take a day off. It's always either working for you or against you. If you're not making your money work, your money is making you work—no matter how little you want to see it.

It can be unthinkably effortless to push our financial plan off to tomorrow. But when we give everything to tomorrow, we just end up with a bunch of empty yesterdays. It's time to act. Kill off your procrastination. The time for tomorrows is gone. We've already decided what we want. Today is the time to go after it—and to keep going after it, day after day.

Commitment doesn't mean much if it's not backed by resilience. Even if you have the highest-octane fuel in your car, if you only fill your tank halfway, you won't make it all the way to the end of the road. You don't just have to dive in. You have to be willing to keep swimming. Otherwise, you'll find that your financial dreams end up half-realized, at best. Many people light up when they have a great business idea. They ride the hype, and spend 100% of their energies on executing their vision—at least, for the first week. But after the work starts, they lose steam.

Here's the thing. It doesn't matter how quickly you get ¼ of the way into the race. You've got to finish the race to enter the ranking. You need a tank full of determination to get to where you want to be.

Financial Freedom

Ideally, money should play one major role in your life. Your finances should make you free. If you feel that your monetary situation is locking you in, whether it's because you have too little money or too much, then it's time to take a step back and assess.

Finance is never one-size-fits-all. Saving money and spending on a budget may not work for some; for others, it can make life simpler and less stressful. You are not living to make money. You're making money to live. True financial freedom focuses your life—it doesn't consume it.

As we continue our discussion of personal and business finances, it's important to keep our eye on the real target. Money isn't the goal. It's a tool.

The Bible tells us that the love of money is the root of all evil, not money itself. Money is like a rope. With money, we can tie things down, lift things up, bind two things together—and, if we're not careful, we can hang ourselves. Like any tool, we can use it to build up or destroy.

Money has the unique ability to increase people in whatever they are. If someone is selfish, more money will make them more selfish. If someone is generous, more money will make them more generous. It's not the money but the character of the person that defines the purpose of finances.

You can have big financial goals without being greedy. You can have a lot of money without looking down on those who don't. You have the power to transform the world, for good or bad.

Avoid the trap that tells you that money is all you need. Balance your financial goals with other priorities in your life. There's nothing wrong with living a well-funded, successful lifestyle, but it's not worth anything if you're miserable, stressed, and worn out. Having more money won't fix problems on its own. It can contribute to your long-term happiness, but you can't measure ultimate satisfaction or fulfillment in your life by the numbers in your bank account.

When we establish our financial vision with purpose and intent, we can live a freer life. We open ourselves up to more options. We're able to enjoy stability, comfort, and happiness. Financial wellness allows us to develop assets that benefit ourselves and the people we love, and to create opportunities that change others' lives for the better.

References for Future Learning

Money Master: The Game by Tony Robbins

Seven Habits of Highly Effective People by Steven Covey

The 80/20 Principle by Richard Koch

The Compound Effect by Darren Hardy

The Million Dollar Real Estate Agent by Gary Keller

The Millionaire Booklet: How to Get Super Rich by Grant Cardone

Time Machine: Five Decisions to Accelerate Your Success Timeline and Live a Thousand Lives by Krish Krohn

Who Not How by Dan Sullivan and Benjamin Hardy

CHAPTER 7

Finances

"We can't be upset by the results we didn't get from the work we didn't do. Don't say, show. Don't promise, prove."

—Jim Kwik

In our previous chapter, we discussed the role of money in our lives. Now that we've established a positive mindset to move us forward financially, it's time to take a closer look at some vital elements of how we get and use our money.

The 4 Phases of Money

If, like many people, it's difficult for you to track your finances, it can feel like money just comes into our lives and leaves whenever it feels like it. Since money is so important in our day-to-day lives, this intangibility can be a source of stress. So, let's make money a little bit more concrete.

Robert Kiyosaki's book *Escape the Rat Race: Learn How Money Works and Become a Rich Kid* is, in my opinion, one of the most simple and basic explanations for how money works. It's an ideal starting place for those getting into financial theory—and, if you listen to the audiobook, you can burn through it in less than an hour. I've gone through that book at least four times over the course of two years.

The rat race that gives Robert Kiyosaki's book its name is the idea that we're trapped in an endless, pointless cycle of earning money, paying off debt and pursuing instant gratification—at which point, we're so broke that we're back to earning money. Breaking out of this cycle is crucial if we want to find financial independence and accrue lasting wealth.

To understand the rat race that we're trying to escape, it's important to gain a deeper understanding of how money comes into and out of our lives. The money cycle can be broken up into 4 stages:

Getting it.
Keeping it.
Investing it.
Spending it.

EARNING

Day Jobs

The first thing I want to tell you about money is that you should keep your day job.

"But Steve!" I hear you cry. "I thought we were talking about financial independence!"

I'll say it again in case you thought it was a misprint: keep your day job.

It doesn't have to be a part of your long-term plan. But keeping your day job for at least two more years is a great way to get financially ahead.

In the financial coaching world, "day job" is sometimes treated as an expletive. Some people believe that your day job takes up valuable hours you should be investing into accruing assets and building your investments. Let's reframe the narrative. When you work for someone else you are essentially being paid to learn some vital life and business lessons. If your goal is to run your own business, you should be taking close notes. Pay attention to the decisions that the executives make. Understand the management structure. Outside of a paycheck position, no one is paid for learning real-life lessons. Use this time to invest in your brain. If you're in a sales or management position, you have the benefit of a contained space with lower stakes—ideal conditions to perfect your communication skills. When you go on to develop your company, you'll be able to easily become a salesman for your own products and a manager of your own team.

Some of you may be planning on sticking with your day-job in the long term, which is just fine. Even if you work a day job, you still have the opportunity to work towards financial independence and to "escape the rat race" through intentional use of your funds. Day jobs are far from financial dead-ends. Pick a company that you're passionate about. Don't be afraid of small companies, either—when you join small businesses, you may get to influence the future direction of the company and the tone of the workplace. Depending on the industry, someone working their way up the ladder could make as much as $100,000 per year after just a small tenure at the company. Additionally, working on W-2 income is the perfect time to focus on building your credit score and borrowing power, which we'll talk more about later in this chapter.

If day jobs are so great, why do so many people warn against them? Well, the pitfall of the day job is that you may end up relying on it as your only stream of income.

A significant facet of financial independence is financial security. This doesn't mean that you don't have to take risks to make money (spoiler: you do). But it does mean that you should use your money to create certain protections, including savings and additional income. These can prevent you from losing your housing situation or living in penny-pinching mode. Relying exclusively on your job for income isn't an ultimately stable plan for your financial future. No matter how good of an employee you are, there's always a chance that you could get laid off or the company could go under. If you're a lifelong employee, even government-backed retirement programs can be unreliable. There's real power in keeping the keys to your financial security close to your chest. Instead, consider additional streams of income that you can start while keeping your day job. I remember setting up my first source of passive income while I was still making active income as an employee.

So, keep your day job. For those looking to escape the employee label, be prepared to quit when the time is right. Don't be afraid to move on when you need to move on. Use your previous experience as a launching pad to move you towards what you want.

Active and Passive Income

There are only two types of income: active and passive.

Active income comes from actively exchanging goods and services for payment. Your day job falls under this umbrella, but so does entrepreneurship and certain types of investment.

On the other hand, you receive passive income when you get money from resources that work for you. This may require work up-front to develop and integrate the resources, such as building a rental unit or finding renters. However, in the long-term, passive income sources require little upkeep but continue to return investments.

When I was calculating my money goals, I kept on running into the same problem. I ran the numbers 10 times. Working by the hour with my restricted wage, I wasn't able to leverage my financial goal into a reality. You can work harder, but under an hourly wage, you're still limited by time.

That's why I started to spend my time building sources of passive income. Rich people don't work for money—their money works for them. Of the businesses I own, I'm actively working on some of them, but, for the most part, I seek passive income through investments. This was a big push towards opening www.steveholm.store, where I sell my personal brand. This is a great example of passive income. After the upfront effort of creating merchandise and YouTube content, I'm able to experience no-effort, long-term reward in sales.

SAVING

There's a concept in the financial world that savers are losers. Robert Kiyosaki, who we've discussed several times in this chapter, is a big pioneer of this concept. He states that people who keep all of their money in the bank are losing money every month. Instead, he recommends that people invest in assets that will return money to them. But don't hop on the train too fast. Savers aren't always losers. In fact, some saving is critical.

Consider what's best for you. Saving your money builds financial security and creates a safety net. Life happens. Emergencies can pop up at any time. Family and personal crises are unpredictable. It's a good idea to consistently save a portion of your money for future use. By keeping a portion of these funds in reserve, they'll be easily available for your use.

It's about balance. As I mentioned, this is a hotly debated topic, so it's a good idea to add it to your list of further research so that you can personally weigh each perspective. Whatever you decide, find a savings amount that works for your life. Think wisely about what you want to put away—and then focus on the money that you want to put to work.

INVESTING

Investing is about putting your money into assets, resources, and ventures that have the potential to grow and generate returns over time. Through strategic investment decisions, you can increase your wealth. Quality investments are the secret to passive income.

There are countless ways to invest, and we'll only touch on a few of them here. Be sure to check out the recommended reading and dive deeper into the investment possibilities.

Real estate is a good example of how active investment often works. Imagine a massive real estate development. You buy a property that's already subdivided from this development. At this point, you build a house on the property and sell it for more than you spent on it, generating profit from the returns. That's one type of investment that qualifies as active income. These types of investments are more valuable than regular active income because the big money is made at the front of the train. You made more money than the general contractor that built the house; the person that you bought the subdivided lot from made even more money than you.

Passive investments are similar, but they tend to return profits for an extended period of time. Consider if you decided to rent the property instead of selling it. The rent that came in for that property would continue until the renters moved out. Both are effective investment models that allow you to get more money for the money that you spent.

Stock Investments

The stock market is often the first thing that people think of when it comes to investments. Many financial giants have made their money buying stocks at low prices and selling them at a double or triple profit.

In Tony Robbins's book *Money Master: The Game,* he discusses stocks, bonds, and mutual funds in depth. This book is a great place to start if you're looking to expand your investments. He recommends seven steps for successful investment, starting by understanding the rules of your specific investment, developing a long-term investment strategy, and learning from top investors to understand and integrate their approach. If you want to pursue stock investments, it's a good idea to dig deep. Research the stocks that you want to buy and pay close attention to the experts. Keep an eye on big stock investors, and don't be afraid to follow their lead.

Instead of making their stocks publicly available, it's worth noting that many companies are opting for private investment. This allows them to target high-money investors, which saves them time and effort. Since private investments are often limited to the financial upper crust, you may not be able to get in on the big stock investments until you've accrued significant wealth. Still, these investments are considered incredibly lucrative.

However, like any industry, the prices of stocks are determined by supply and demand. Stocks in high demand cost more and vis versa. As a result, stocks are notoriously erratic. Personally, I only put a little bit of money into stocks. I'm only willing to put in as much as I can afford to lose.

Risk Management

Stocks aren't the only investments with risk, though they may be the most well-known. Just like a valuable investment can return significant profits, an investment that goes south can become a serious loss.

Grant Cardone's book *The Millionaire Booklet* stresses the importance of generating multiple streams of income to safeguard against financial instability. He warns against putting all of your eggs into one basket. When you prioritize only a few investments by pouring a significant amount of your money into them, you put yourself at risk for a disaster if the investments fall through. Instead, you need multiple streams of investment income—that way, even if the basket falls, you'll still have some unbroken eggs. Be cautious, start small, and plan for diversification as soon as you can. As Warren Buffet, an American businessman, investor, and philanthropist, said, "Rule number 1 is don't lose money. Rule number 2 is don't forget rule number 1."

Maximizing wealth accumulation through your investments means that you have to take calculated risks and actively seek out opportunities. In his book, Cardone emphasizes the importance of persistence, perseverance, and continued education to remain competitive and safeguarded in the constantly changing financial landscape. It's important to be strategic and minimize risk, but don't let fear or uncertainty hold you back from potential success. Start small, but don't be afraid to invest. It could be the first crucial step toward financial freedom.

SPENDING

Financial independence requires financial responsibility. The final stage of money is all about utilizing saved and invested money to meet current expenses, fulfill financial goals, enjoy experiences, and improve your quality of life and the world around you.

This is where some people propose a budget. In my personal life, I don't budget. I find that budgeting forces me into a poverty mindset, and it doesn't bring value to my life. I may not run completely wild and free—but I don't restrict myself to a budget that I made a month ago because of the way my income may adjust.

It's all about finding the right balance for you between spending, saving, and investing. As you continue to research these topics and enact change in your life, you'll be well on your way to financial stability.

Utilizing Debt

The debt debate is the most controversial topic in the financial field. Some believe that debt is to be avoided at all costs. Dave Ramsey said, “Debt is not a tool. It is a method to make banks wealthy, not you.” Similarly, Henry Wheeler Shaw said, “Debt is like any other trap. Easy enough to get into, but hard enough to get out of.” Even Robert Kiyosaki, a billionaire who keeps going viral for being in increasingly severe debt, said, “Good debt is a powerful tool, but bad debt can kill you.”

Yet debt is one thing that many famous companies have in common. As of September 2023, the famous Apple company is $111 billion in debt; Microsoft, $71 billion; Harley-Davidson, $7.9 billion; Walgreens, $8.1 billion; Cisco, $6.6 billion; Costco Wholesale, $6.4 billion; Walmart, $69.7 billion; American Express, $48 billion; Google, $26.3 billion.

The United States’ debt adds up to more than $100,000 for every person who lives in the country. That means a total of $34.7 trillion in debt.

If you have followed the narrative that debt = financial insecurity, these numbers are staggering. But the pattern that’s shown here isn’t necessarily a bad thing.

Let’s take a look at the anti-debt crowd. Dave Ramsey is a strong advocate against debt. One of his big points is that debt could put you at risk. If, for example, you suddenly left your job or had an income-halting emergency, you wouldn’t have a way to pay back your debts. He argues against donating to charities or making risky financial decisions until you are completely debt-free.

This may be valuable advice—although, I couldn’t help but notice that Dave often writes about millionaires. When you start looking into billionaires, you begin to see incredible amounts of debt. These billionaires leverage their debt to further their finances.

Not all debt is created equal. There's a big difference between a credit card addict's debt and an investor's debt. The one falls into debt to get every single thing they think they want—the other uses debt to buy profitable investments. Tony Robbins, Kris Krohn, Grant Cardone, and Robert Kiyosaki are great resources for those looking for more information on how to leverage debt in a beneficial way.

Be cautious when taking on non-investment debts. Low-interest loans, like those available for many vehicles, can be a double-sided sword. Loans with 0% interest offer what seems to be free money, since inflation is ruining the dollar at more than 0%. However, these kinds of loans often factor in additional transaction fees. I once saw a Polaris snowmobile on a website that offered either a 0% loan on a sled or a three-year warranty that cost an extra $2,000. In other words, they had simply rolled the interest into the purchase price. These kinds of scams are common ways for companies to trick customers into believing they're getting a deal, and taking on debt that doesn't serve them.

Building Credit

When it comes to leveraging your debt for good, your credit is king. Building your credit is a work of years. Over a course of time, you have to prove that you can consistently pay things off that were credited—which you can't do without debt. Once you prove consistency and reliability through smaller debts, lenders can use your credit score to give you larger loans, which can be used for more valuable investments.

Building credit is an important step for managing your long-term finances. Even if you don't want to borrow right now, it may be in your cards later on. Keeping your credit score up prepares you for your potential financial future.

The easiest way to start building your credit is to open a credit card account. Use the card for small, regular purchases, such as gas or groceries, then pay the balance in full each month. Another way to begin building credit is to take out a small loan, such as a personal or car loan, and then be sure to meet your payments on time. It may not seem like a big deal, but missing one payment can leave a mark on your credit that takes a long time to scrub out.

Building credit takes time. Be patient and consistent.

Here are some additional tips for building your credit and increasing your borrower power:

Pay bills on time. This includes credit card bills, utility bills, and loan payments. Your credit score is partially affected by percentages. If you've made 100 payments and 10 of them were late, that means that 90% of your payments were on time. You can work to raise this number by making many more on-time payments, but it takes time for the percentage to adjust. It's best to start paying your bills on time as soon as possible.

Keep credit utilization low. Try to keep your credit card balances low. Aim to use less than 9% of the available credit. Higher credit utilization ratios may indicate higher credit risk, which could lower your credit score. This percentage is checked on the statement date. Be sure to check the statement date and keep that 9% threshold.

Diversify your credit. Consider maintaining a mix of credit accounts such as credit cards, installment loans, and mortgages. When you manage a variety of credit types, you demonstrate an ability to keep up with different kinds of debt. This is a part of the difference between your credit score and your "borrowing power." The terms are related, but your credit score is a number assigned from the credit bureaus to reflect how well you pay your payments. Meanwhile, borrowing power shows how well you manage multiple loans at a time, and how often you close loans by paying them in full. Both are important for qualifying for loans and securing financing.

Monitor your credit score. Regularly check your credit report from all three major credit bureaus: Equifax, Experion, and TransUnion. This way, you can monitor for fraud and inaccuracies. Disputing these can help you maintain a clean credit report. A variety of apps are available so that you can monitor your credit without paying exorbitant fees.

Build a long credit history. The longer your recorded history, the more trustworthy you seem. Avoid closing old credit card accounts—these contribute to the average length of your credit history.

Explore different ways to improve credit. For example, at the time I'm writing this, there's something called the Extra Debit card, which allows you to make payments for small charges, raising the total payments made on time to decrease the percentage of missed payments. New opportunities to improve your credit will continue to arise, so be sure to keep a pulse on these developments by following them online and in the news.

One day, I ran the numbers on the insurance for my truck. I found that, over the course of one year, I could save $600 by putting all of the insurance for the year on a credit card for 20% interest in comparison with paying the insurance monthly. Of course, this was about $1,200 more expensive than it would have been to pay in-cash upfront. However, by using a credit card, I was able to pay less for my insurance while building my credit at the same time. These sorts of situations are surprisingly common. It's a good idea to consistently run the numbers on your regular expenses and think outside the box for ways to build your credit while saving money.

Investors and Interest

Compound interest is a foundational concept when it comes to your investments. When you have a profitable investment, you receive interest from it. You can pocket that interest—or you can choose to put that earned interest back into the investment. This gives you the potential to increase the next sum of interest that you'll get from the investment. The interest gained from this cycle of depositing and accumulating funds is compound interest.

The rule of 72 is an important guide for compound interest. With one percent of compounding interest, you will double your money in 72 years. That means, if you make 10% compound interest, you will double your money in 7.2 years. This acts as a practical guideline for understanding the power of compound interest and increasing the return of your investments.

Similarly, we follow a loose 1% rule in rentals. You should expect to make a monthly return on your investment of about 1% of the original investment value. That means if you bought a $100,000 house, you'd want to rent it for $1,000 per month, assuming that the interest rate is below 7-8% APR. If the interest rate is about 5% for every $100,000 borrowed from the bank, you should look to make at least $650 in rental income. This offers a base to calculate potential return on investments. A $300,000 house should be rented out for a minimum of $1950 per month to reach this goal, and so forth.

Another quick number we use when it comes to commercial rental spaces is one dollar per square foot base number. So, a $10,000 square-foot shop would rent for $10,000 a month, plus or minus additional perks or rental needs.

These are just rough guidelines developed by investors. If you're struggling to wade through the financial mumbo-jumbo, no worries. Simply add compound interest and return interest to your research list. If these types of investments come up as a part of your future financial plan, you can return to this section, then dive into deeper research from there with additional books and online resources. Chances are, these numbers won't stay still—make sure to stay up-to-date on the market that you're looking to invest in.

Cash Flow

Cash flow is simply the amount of money that comes in and out of a business, but it can also be applied to your personal finances. One of Robert Kiyosaki's tenets is that cash flow is vital.

My first real estate deal was a small half-acre property from a friend. He agreed to sell it to me for $90,000. It was about ten minutes away from my workplace, so I made a deal with my coworkers. I would live on the property, and they could rent bedrooms in the house. I'd be responsible for the loan and my own portion of the payment. But when I broke down the numbers, I found that money from my renters would cover the entire mortgage payment. I had another coworker who had an RV. He rented a spot on my property for it. I had a plumber add another connection and got an electrician to add another plug. Since the renters in the house were covering the mortgage payment, all of the money I received from the RV rental was profit. I was not only living for free—I was making money. In the first year, I was making $800 per month.

This was all extra cash flow. I used this to pay off the mortgage sooner, shortening my loan and limiting the interest.

I understand—not everyone can find a $90,000 rental property. However, there are dozens of simple and creative ways to increase your cash flow. Consider investing in a vending machine or billboard. Tell your work friends that you'd pick them up a coffee on your lunch break if they'd pay you an extra dollar. If you found ten friends willing to pay you for coffee delivery, that's an extra $10 a day. That's $50 extra dollars for a standard work week, and $200 extra dollars for the month.

The rich make connections. The poor have excuses.

Taxes

If someone were to ask me how much I pay in income taxes, my reply would have to be, "Why would I pay income taxes?"

Taxes are the average person's largest expense in life. However, for above-average people, taxes are a non-issue. It's true—rich people don't pay taxes, because rich people play by the rules. The tax code was written to benefit those who stimulate the economy—i.e., those who have high cash flow. If you tax the rich too much, they might just hop in their private jets and fly away, taking the nation's economy with them. So, they get tax breaks. The largest tax breaks are for people who own land and real estate. The second largest tax breaks are for companies. Business supplies income for employees, which keeps the economy moving.

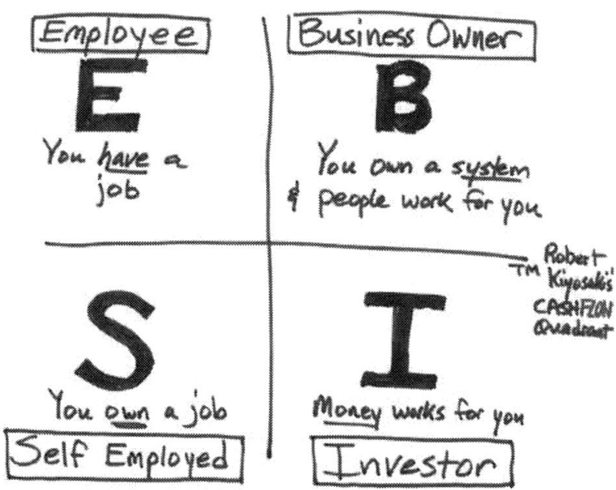

In the illustration above, I borrowed from Robert Kiyosaki's Cash Flow Quadrant.

The Cash Flow Quadrant has four sections for the four different types of people in the financial world. In the top left corner, we have employees who are in the worst possible tax bracket. In the bottom left corner, we have those who are self-employed, who are in a slightly better tax bracket. On the upper right corner, we'll find business owners, and then, in the lower right corner, investors, who are in the best tax brackets. You'll notice that those who are in the most lucrative tax brackets are also the ones who experience the most cash flow.

When you stop spending money on consumption and start spending money on making money, the tax code rewards you.

This is how quitting my day job saved me money on taxes. When the time was right, I quit my 6-figure, W-2 income job and started a side business working for the same hourly rate. I immediately got a 24% raise. My company started to pay for my expenses. I was able to write off everything as a loss. On paper, my company didn't make money. It is 100% legal, and I paid *no* taxes. I highly recommend looking up Kiyosaki's cash flow quadrant for more information about how our taxes interact with our cash flow.

This is a great way to work around taxes as a full-fledged business owner, but you don't have to own a business to play the game. If possible, ask your employer if you can work on a 1099 instead of a W-2, subcontracting on the same hourly rate that you currently work. Under this income, you can start your own "business." If your employers greenlight this, then you can start writing off your expenses to avoid taxation.

Sales

Everything comes down to sales.

Your ability to sell is particularly important if you're a business owner or if you are in a customer-facing position. However, persuasion is a vital life skill that can have a significant impact on your finances. Maybe you're selling a product or service. Maybe you're selling your spouse on a new idea. Maybe you're selling yourself as a credible option for the new promotion.

A fantastic resource for learning selling skills is Dr. Robert B. Cialdini's *The Psychology of Persuasion.* In this book, Dr. Cialdini provides several practical tips for persuading others, from leveraging your authority to highlighting scarcity. One of the major messages of his book is ethical persuasion. When we understand persuasive methods, we can use them to influence others in a positive and ethical way. It's not about trying to squeeze people into buying an overpriced product. Sales skills are the very best in the hands of those who want to make the world a better place. You can have genuine and honorable intentions and be a persuasive communicator. It's all about connecting with other people to give them something that will make their life better.

Former FBI negotiator Chris Voss wrote *Never Split the Difference,* a powerful book about negotiation that applies directly to sales power. He focuses on the importance of connecting with others' perspectives and emotions, then finding the right ways to approach an individual and asking them the right questions during negotiation. It's an excellent book for improving your persuasive skills in both personal and professional settings, which fundamental to the skill of selling.

Selling is all about understanding what your customers want. Good sellers get paid for connecting dots that no one else has connected—whether you're connecting a customer to a product or a spouse to an idea. Just like interpersonal communication, sales are multifaceted. Most expert salesmen take years to develop their skills. Be sure to check out the wealth of online information on sales and persuasion.

Financial Management

Over the past two chapters, we've covered a few important topics to give you an overview of personal and business finances. I hope this will be an effective introductory guide to the world of money. These foundational principles are the basis for reaching your financial goals.

References for Future Learning

Escape the Rat Race: Learn How Money Works and Become a Rich Kid by Robert Kiyosaki

Never Split the Difference by Chris Voss

Rich Dad's Cashflow Quadrant: Guide to Financial Freedom by Robert Kiyosaki

Sell or be Sold: How to Get Your Way in Business and in Life by Grant Cardone

The Holy Grail of Investing by Tony and Christopher Zook

The Psychology of Persuasion by Robert B. Cialdini

The Total Money Makeover by Dave Ramsey

CHAPTER 8

Leadership

"Be the leader you with you had."

—Simon Sinek

About three months ago, I had a thought while I was driving down the road. Every organization that is based on correct principles can never be destroyed from the outside.

This applies to families, businesses, church organizations, and even countries. The United States couldn't be truly taken down by an outside force—there isn't enough nuclear power in the world to destroy the doctrines of this country. As long as there were people who abided by constitutional principles, the United States would be alive and strong. If, however, the corruption came from the inside, and those principles were abandoned, the United States would immediately begin to collapse.

In our lives, we should focus on reinforcing our internal framework. Internal strength creates a fortress that can weather all external opposition. And those who bolster, uphold, and defend the correct principles at the heart of the organization? Those are the leaders.

Take a moment to think of a failed business that appeared to be sturdy. Maybe it had gone through a tough time or two, but it always seemed to get back up on its feet. Then, suddenly, it started to fall apart. In most cases, this happens because of a decay in internal leadership. The upper-level administration began to neglect the mission of the business, lost discipline, or became greedy. The decay doesn't come out of nowhere—it starts at the very center of the organization: the leaders.

In this chapter, we're going to discuss the importance of being a strong leader, no matter what professional role you fill. We'll briefly talk about solving problems as a leader and inspiring others to create change.

Lead at Every Level

Alvin Harker, project manager at Innovatech and a personal friend of mine, once told me, "Culture will eat strategy for lunch at the workplace."

We've already discussed the importance of strategy at length (see Chapter 4). As for culture? When you're willing to become a leader, you have the ability to drastically affect your workplace culture, whether you're a CEO, a grunt worker, or anything in-between. Leaders are willing to connect with those around them and spread their positivity. They become a leader by being ready, willing, and approachable. It makes their voice heard, even if they're sitting in a crowded room. You can even become a leader to your co-workers. You just need to become someone who they can come to for advice, direction, and encouragement.

In an interview uploaded to his YouTube channel, business leadership expert Simon Sinek said, "The middle management team is stuck between strategic and tactical thinking—they're the translator between the two." Those in this position don't get to make the big decisions, but they have to deal with the backlash. "Most things," Simon continued, "break in the middle."

When I heard this speech, I was actually working as a middle manager at a large manufacturing company. It hit me hard. I realized that I needed to approach my work from a different way.

Luckily, Simon presents a solution. These people in the middle—the people who have leadership thrust upon them—need to be taught important leadership skills: listening, communication, effective confrontation, and giving and receiving feedback. These skills are what elevate a manager—or, for that matter, a front-line worker—to a leader. When we choose to develop leadership skills and lead at our level, we can influence our culture for the better, whether it's at work or within our families. Simon Sinek offers several solutions for learning how to listen to and empathize with others. Consider finding him online or on YouTube to learn more.

Leading for Solutions

One of the greatest signs of a leader is that they work to solve problems, not create them. When you have a solution-oriented mindset (see Chapter 5), you lead groups to resolve problems and seek collaboration.

Leaders should be able to cut to the heart of a problem. While interpersonal disagreements are complicated, here is a small guide to identifying the root cause during conflict resolution. Try utilizing these questions the next time you want to stretch your leadership muscles.

Business connections. Analyze whether the challenge is with the relationship between the two parties, or if the problem is with money. Has something changed in the relationship dynamic? Has there been a breakdown in communication? Or is there simply a lack of funds?

Personal relationships. Consider if the problem is in the connection between the two parties, or if there's a problem with follow-through. Are the two people facing fundamental problems in how they think? Or is there just a problem with fulfilling their commitments to each other?

After identifying the main conflict, you can work constructively to develop mutually beneficial solutions.

Developing Leadership Skills

Leaders create big change through their interpersonal skills. In Dale Carnegie's *How to Win Friends and Influence People,* he shares practical tools for creating mutually beneficial relationships and leading others. The leadership skills that he highlights include inspiring others and leading by example. Many of the skills that we've developed in this book so far apply to leadership. When you foster a positive mindset, you create an environment that draws others to you. When you have a nuanced perspective on life, you can make strong decisions for yourself and your team. By creating these changes within ourselves and focusing on our leadership potential, we'll find that others will be eager to follow.

References for Future Learning

How to Win Friends and Influence People by Dale Carnegie

"Why Middle Management is the Hardest Job | Simon Sinek," from YouTube channel *Simon Sinek*

CHAPTER 9

Health

"Take care of your body. It's the only place you have to live."

—Jim Rohn

Think over everything we've covered in this book so far. Imagine that you've developed all the characteristics that we've discussed. You have a positive mindset, a nuanced perspective, a strategic vision for your future, and excellent financial habits.

How valuable are these things if your body is breaking down?

What good is money if you can't enjoy it with a beautiful life? What good is fame if your health won't let you enjoy it?

We experience the world through our bodies. Our health is a significant defining factor in how we feel. The state of our health influences our emotional wellness, capabilities, mental capacity, and much more. Good health isn't just a convenience. In this fast-paced world, it's a necessity. It's the foundation on which we base our lives.

When we maintain our health, we're able to enjoy the activities we love. A healthy lifestyle allows you to pursue your passions without limitations. It removes barriers by enabling you to tackle life's challenges with energy and enthusiasm. Plus, prioritizing health now may prevent chronic disease and disability in the future. Imagine a life where you wake up feeling energized, motivated, and ready to start your day. That's the power of good health, and it's essential for thriving physically, mentally, and emotionally.

Good health directly translates to increased productivity and better performance. It enables you to be a more efficient worker, a more dedicated student, and a more supportive friend, partner, and parent. A healthy body is even better able to maintain the right mindset (see Chapter 1). As John F. Kennedy said, "Physical fitness is not only one of the most important keys to a healthy body. It is the basis of dynamic and creative intellectual activity." When your body and mind have what they need to function optimally, you can excel in your personal and professional pursuits.

Just like we did with our finances, we need to start by analyzing how we perceive our health. How do you define "health?" Is good health just the absence of illness?

As a society, we're taught that average health and good health are the same thing. So long as there are no red flags popping up during your examination, most doctors send you home with a clean bill of health. But this conceptualization of health can hold us back. If we strive not only to meet the bare minimum, but, instead, to become the healthiest versions of ourselves, we will unlock our true capacities.

We should begin to think about our health as an investment. Establishing healthy habits is investing in a future with less disease, more energy, and a higher quality of life. Your health is your most valuable asset, and in the long run, it gives you the best returns.

Maintaining Good Health

When it comes to healthcare, it's easy to get overwhelmed. It doesn't take much research before it becomes clear that there are a thousand different specific subjects, with hundreds of professional opinions on each. It can be difficult to find relevant advice for your personal wellness in the sea of medical studies, jargon, and research.

Bias from specialists can also steer you in the wrong direction. I realized that, when I walked into a chiropractor's office, an adjustment would fix all of my issues. When I walked into a dentist's office, my jaw and teeth would mean the difference between good and bad health. When I walked into a Health Food store, a good diet would ward off every illness. This can be confusing and misleading. In reality, health is a combination of many different components. Your health is a 12-sided die, and it's important that you don't favor one element over others.

Each area of your body requires specialized care, and each person is different. What works for one may not work for another. As we continue our discussion, consider your specific lifestyle, and account for challenges that you've had with your health in the past.

For the rest of this chapter, we're going to take a closer look at some important areas of your health, discuss some relevant tips, and review resources to guide your future research. This brief overview provides some essential information that may be useful as you develop a routine that best fits your personal needs.

ORGAN HEALTH

Your vital organs (your heart, brain, kidneys, liver, and lungs) require special care. Caring for your organ systems, vital and non-vital alike, is a crucial step to improving your overall wellness. These organs are the engine behind your life—it's a good idea to keep them in tune.

Your heart pumps at least 100,000 times a day without you even noticing. I don't know about you, but it's the most incredible pump that I've ever heard of. If you live one hundred years, your heart will pump something like

182,500,000 gallons of blood in the course of your life. Similarly, our lungs are constantly circulating air. On their own, our cardiovascular and respiratory systems are responsible for our most foundational life support—and we don't even have to think about it.

Over time, even these incredible pumps begin to wear out. However, through proactive maintenance, we can extend the lifespan of our organs.

Regular exercise, along with other positive health habits, can improve your organ health. Try to prioritize stress management, as heavy stress can negatively affect several organ systems, and consider ways to protect your body from undue strain. There are many small habits that you can integrate to improve your organ health. For example, you can actually perfect the way that you breathe. James Nestor wrote an entire book about developing healthy breathing habits, called *Breath: The New Science of a Lost Art.* Similarly, you can try to give your eyes—one of your sensory organs—a break from screens and protect your vision from UV rays by wearing sunglasses. If you're interested in protecting your eyes, be sure to look up the effects of light on your eyesight. Avoid excessive exposure to loud noises to protect your ears—another sensory organ—to maintain your hearing. These small changes can make a big difference to your organ health in the long run. Dr. Andrew Huberman's videos are a great place to start if you want more detailed information about caring for your organ health.

HORMONAL HEALTH

No matter your age, your hormones play a significant role in your emotional regulation and overall health. Your endocrine system, the network of glands that produce hormones, influences an incredible array of your bodily functions.

Your reproductive health is one of the most significant factors influenced by your hormones. Like any medical issue, reproductive health is multi-faceted. However, there are a few factors that apply to most individuals. First and foremost is that your reproductive health is often a reflection of your overall health. If your body is healthy, you're more likely to have good reproductive health. For those who are actively working towards children, now is the time to create healthy habits. The health habits you make today will influence their lives in the future.

There are several common threats to your reproductive health today. Cell phones are probably the most well-known. If you keep your phone near your genitals, it could affect your reproductive health at a cellular level.

Related to your endocrine system is your lymphatic system, which removes excess hormones, toxins, and waste from your body. Proper lymphatic drainage is important—but many people struggle with proper lymphatic function and don't even know it.

Once, I was talking to a doctor about a friend of mine who struggles with obesity. He was several hundred pounds overweight, and it was severely affecting his health. The doctor told me that my friend may have had as much as 50 pounds of residual waste piling up in his lymphatic system. Not only was this contributing to his weight—it was making him *feel* worse.

By encouraging proper lymphatic drainage, we can optimize our bodies. Flushing the garbage away will often make us feel better—and may even shave off a few extra pounds.

One easy technique for increasing your lymphatic drainage is to place your hands on the sides of your head, splitting your fingers so that they don't touch your ears. Then, move your fingers around in slow circles, pressing down as much as you comfortably can. Then, move your hands down to the top of your should or the base of your neck and press five more circles there, then repeat the process inside each armpit. To finish, use your hands to "push" the drainage down towards your kidneys. These simple behaviors can stimulate lymphatic drainage.

Luckily, there are ways for you to encourage lymphatic drainage, right at home. I have one easy technique. Start by placing your hands on the sides of your head, splitting your fingers so that you don't cover your ears. Then, press your fingers lightly into your scalp, and move your fingers around in slow circles. After tracing these circles about five times, move your hands down to the top of your shoulders or the base of your neck, pressing your fingers into the area and making five circles into your skin. Repeat this process inside each armpit. Lastly, use your palms to "push" the drainage down, in the direction of your kidneys.

This is just one method—there are dozens of other tips and tricks for stimulating lymphatic drainage. Another popular option is to use a soft brush, dragging it from your knees towards your bladder. Others prefer to jump on a trampoline or use a vibration plate to create movement in their bodies. Experiment with different ways to encourage drainage and consider integrating it into your daily routine to keep your bodily systems flowing smoothly.

DIET AND DIGESTIVE HEALTH

Diet has far-reaching effects for your health. Eating poorly can easily snowball into an increasingly dangerous crisis. Those with poor diets might get away with it for six months without any effects. The lucky ones might get away with it for several years. But no one gets away with it forever.

What you put in is what you get out. When you put bad fuel into your body, your body can only deliver poor results. When you put good fuel into your body, your body can generate remarkable results. Take time to explore the right dietary options for you to optimize your health. One great resource for understanding more about diet and health is *Food Fix* by Mark Hyman. This book provides a fantastic overview of the way that food impacts our personal health and our communities.

Weight management is another important topic that dominates the healthcare community. A healthy diet, even more than excessive exercise, is important for sustainably maintaining a healthy weight. Extreme exercise for weight loss can actually harm your body. If those who are overweight take up excessive jogging, for example, they can cause significant damage to their knees and legs. You have to consider the best way to balance your diet and your exercise to achieve your health goals.

But diet has far-reaching consequences beyond your weight. Since our body acts as a complex ecosystem, issues with our diet can have ramifications across several different systems. Eating too many fatty foods can cause liver damage, and a diet high in salt can affect our kidney function. The book *Jaws* by Sandra Kahn and Paul R. Ehrlich goes into detail about how the food that we eat even influences the development of our jaws.

MUSCULAR HEALTH

Here's a little exercise. Stop where you are, right now, and check your posture. If you're like most, you might find that your back is hunched, and your shoulders are uneven. Particularly for those who work an office job, this posture is all too easy to slip into.

Posture is important for preventing muscle pain and injury, particularly in your back and neck. Poor posture takes its toll on your body by degrees. It may take decades for the full consequences of your posture to hit you. Alternatively, maintaining good posture as a habit bolsters your muscular health and prevents pain in the long- and short-term.

A variety of therapies focus on easing muscle strain to reduce stress and improve overall health. Zone therapy or reflexology is one alternative medical practice that focuses on certain points on the feet and hands to improve whole-body wellness. Consider looking into reflexology and similar therapies online—it's amazing to understand how one part of your body can have such a significant impact on the rest.

We can't address muscular health without talking about exercise. Regular exercise is an important part of maintaining flexibility and movement. Exercise empowers your personal agency while improving your health. When you increase your physical strength, you may find that your perception of yourself improves. You may gain additional self-confidence through your physique.

When it comes to exercise, like diet, it's all about experimenting to find what works for you. Personally, I prefer calisthenics over heavy lifting—I find that it maximizes my flexibility while developing the strength I need for body and weight exercises.

If you have the time and you're willing to put in the effort, you can work pretty much any muscle in your body to gain definition and strength. There are even tools like the gyroscope wheel which focuses on developing the muscles in your forearms. Whatever you want to focus on, there are tools and resources for you.

SKELETAL AND JOINT HEALTH

Poor posture doesn't just affect our musculature. It's also incredibly hard on our spine. James Levine, a professor of medicine at the Mayo Clinic, said, "Sitting is the new smoking." Excessive and improper sitting is a widespread pandemic that is drastically affecting our health. Life coach

Tony Robbins even encourages us to think about sitting as a sport—something we can train at and perfect. When we spend a good portion of our day sitting down, we need to make sure that we're doing it the right way. This will mitigate the damage to our bones and joints.

Additionally, try to incorporate regular exercises to improve your joint health. Your joints end up with a ton of stress and strain. Intensive jobs like welding and grinding involve heavy vibrations that can damage your wrists—but even office jobs can wear away at our wrists. To prevent carpal tunnel, take a few minutes every day to perform wrist stretches. Similarly, yoga can improve your joint health and heighten your flexibility. Mobility focuses on improving your range of motion to strengthen your joints and muscles. In this way, it helps you maintain balance and stability. Seek out resources online to find stretching and yoga routines that you can do to improve your joint health. YouTuber *MovementbyDavid* is a favorite of mine for mobility and strength training. Another YouTube resource that is great for mobility is user *TheKneesOverToesGuy*.

Additionally, it's important to consider how each skeletal system is unique. You may have different needs than others, and this can influence your exercise routine, your supplements—and even your footwear.

Once, I was playing basketball while wearing $300 signature basketball shoes. Expensive and built for the sport. I'd figured those would do the trick, right?

Wrong. While we were playing, I jumped up to block someone from a shot. When I came down, I landed right on someone's foot and rolled my ankle. It went black and blue. It took months for my ankle to fully heal.

The fancy, expensive shoes weren't the right kind of shoe for my foot. When I finally got back to playing, I bought some

$180 shoes that fit my foot shape much better. Since then, I haven't had a problem.

These kinds of minute changes can make a big difference in our overall health, and work to prevent injury or pain in the long-term.

MENTAL HEALTH

Your mind is your greatest resource. A healthy life must include mental health. Your emotional wellness plays a significant role in how you feel, and it can even affect other areas of your health. Be sure to reflect on the mental health practices that we discussed in Chapter 1 to maintain a positive mindset. Prioritize your mental wellness so that you can be empowered to reach your goals.

Additionally, it's a good idea to train your mind to think adaptively and creatively. Your mind can be trained like any muscle. Stay mentally active with puzzles. Read new books. Challenge your brain to keep it at the top of its game. It's the most important tool you have. As I've emphasized in this illustration, one of the best places that you can work out is the library.

Your mind can be trained like any muscle. Stay mentally active with puzzles. Read new books. Seek out stimulating activities. Training your brain doesn't always have to be complex—some exercises require simple movements.

Here is one straightforward exercise that can fine-tune your mind. Bring both of your hands up to rest flat in front of you. Then, lift both of your hands ten inches in the air—but try to make one of your hands go up and down twice in the time it takes your other hand to make the loop.

This is just one example of the myriad of ways we can work to keep our brains acute. For more ways to sharpen your mind, I highly recommend brain coach Jim Kwik's YouTube channel and similar resources.

SLEEP

I've included an entire section on sleep because of the massive role it plays in your overall health. In reality, I could write an entire chapter or an entire book on the power of sleep—which many people already have. A few of my favorite books on sleep are *Limitless: Upgrade Your Brain, Learn Anything Faster, and Unlock Your Exceptional Life* by Jim Kwik, *Why We Sleep* by Matthew Walker, and *Sleep Smarter* by Shawn Stevenson. These are all great books to read for in-depth information on the importance of sleep and developing healthy sleep habits. For now, we'll touch on some of the most important ideas related to sleep and health.

Sleep improves your memory, cognitive skills, creative abilities, and decision-making skills. It can also improve your attention span. A good night's rest makes you better prepared to modulate your mood and manage stress and anxiety. As a result, sleep can improve your relationships with others. Sleep also has a quantifiable effect on your physical wellness, regulating your appetite and weight, strengthening your immune system, and even lowering your risk of chronic diseases.

If you're looking to get better sleep, here are some tips and tricks that I've accrued over time. Look these over—though they may not be for you, they may be a good stepping off point to take you in the right direction.

1. Stick to a consistent sleep schedule. Go to bed and wake up at the same time every day, even on weekends. A consistent sleep schedule is critical to a healthy circadian rhythm.

2. Create a relaxing bedtime routine. Making a habit of reading, taking a warm bath, or meditating before bed. When you start these habits, you'll signal to your body that it's time to sleep. For best results, put away the electronics at least an hour before you go to sleep, or at least turn on blue-light settings to reduce eye strain.

3. Adjust the environment. Make sure that your bedroom is conducive to sleep by keeping it cool, dark, and quiet. Invest in a supportive mattress, quality pillows, and breathable bedding. Ideally, your room should be about 5° colder when you go to sleep than when you wake up. There are mattresses out there that offer time-based heating and cooling, but you don't need one to create this effect. Try sleeping with the back of your upper neck on an ice pack. In two or so hours, the ice will melt. By the time you wake up, your body will be slightly warmer than when you went to sleep.

4. Watch your habits. Exercising regularly can improve your sleep, though you should avoid exercising at least one hour before sleep to allow your body time to comfortably wind down. Additionally, you'll want to steer clear of heavy meals or excessive fluids close to sleep. You may also want to incorporate mindful habits to manage stress like deep breathing, meditation, or yoga. If you struggle to sleep at night, be sure to limit daytime napping, particularly in the late afternoon or evening.

And we've only skimmed the surface. Sleep is highly complex, and it's been a point of study for centuries. There are dozens of subtopics to explore—like earthing or sleep grounding, which simulates sleeping on the ground outside for surprising health benefits. For more in-depth information on sleep, I recommend Dr. Andrew Huberman's podcast, *Huberman Lab*. Remember, the internet is a phenomenal resource. You can find fantastic resources for more information on nearly every subject of your health and wellness, and sleep is no exception.

Explore New Treatments

In *Abundance: The Future is Better Than You Think*, authors Peter Diamandis and Steven Kotlers explore how advances in technology could solve some of the world's most pressing challenges. Today, we are developing new tools that could prepare us to address poverty, disease, and environmental degradation. This book highlights an important truth: we are living in an age of unprecedented abundance. Innovations like artificial intelligence, biotechnology, and renewable energy are constantly being refined.

It's true; we live on the cutting edge of medical knowledge. New research is constantly revealing unique and innovative solutions to age-old health problems. It's tempting to stick with the time-tested health solutions, but the world is changing. To cultivate the best health practices, you've got to keep an eye on the up-and-coming treatments.

One of the most promising treatments is stem cell therapy. While it's been in development for decades, it's recently gained traction for its exceptional results. Stem cell therapy is a regenerative form of therapy. It works by promoting the repair response of injured tissue using stem cells, which can develop into many different types of cells for use all around the body. Stem cell therapy may restore proper function across several organ systems as well as extend the longevity of healthy organs. There are even supplements that you can take to bolster the extant stem cells in your lungs. It's not just limited to your vital organs. Tony Robbins discusses his experience with stem cell therapy in his book *Lifeforce*. He was suffering from an incapacitating rotating cuff injury. Through stem cell therapy, he was able to recover in only three weeks.

Another area that is experiencing drastic advancements is that of longevity. If you want to see one of the youngest old people alive, check out Dr. David Sinclair. Start by taking a look at his picture—you'll see a man who looks somewhere in his early thirties, max. You'd never believe that he was 55 years old.

Dr. Sinclair's book *Lifespan: Why We Age—and Why We Don't Have To* is an in-depth look into the science of aging. Sinclair is a renowned geneticist and leading expert in the field of aging research. He presents groundbreaking theories about ways that we can slow the aging process to extend our lifespan. Sinclair proposes that aging is not an inevitable process, but rather a malleable one. He suggests several interventions that may reduce the effects of age, including caloric restrictions, intermittent fasting, and supplementation. New research is further revealing how lifestyle factors such as diet, exercise, and stress can all affect our biological age and overall health. Even more dramatic treatments are on the rise, including epigenetics, which are DNA modifications that may allow us to influence how our genes are expressed and, ultimately, how we age.

These are just a few of the amazing possibilities that we're facing. Within the next few years, we're sure to see a dozen more medical breakthroughs. Let's keep our minds open to new methodologies and keep an eye out for new research. Even one five-minute Google search can reveal the life-changing marvels of modern medicine.

Create Healthy Habits

As we reviewed different areas of health, you may have noticed a re-occurring theme. There were no one-stop solutions. When it comes to improving our health in the long-term, it's not about the quick fixes. True, sustainable health is in our habits.

Integrating even one healthy habit can radically affect your whole-body health. Consider dehydration. Dehydration is a massive issue—many people are dehydrated without even realizing it. By hydrating properly, you can benefit from a myriad of effects. Hydration improves your mental wellness, aids in organ function, defends you from disease, and can even help you lose weight. Your brain, your liver, your kidneys, and more are all improved by this one habit.

Similarly, negative habits can wear down on your health in many ways. Just like hydrating properly can improve your overall wellness, drinking alcohol can damage your body at every level. Smoking—even second-hand smoking—can cause a chain-reaction of damage in multiple organ systems. When you choose to limit your drinking and stop smoking, you benefit your lungs, your throat, your heart, your mental wellness, and much more.

By committing to healthy habits, we can work to target the source of our ailments, rather than the symptoms. Take split ends. Trimming off your unhealthy hair won't make it grow back stronger. The easiest way to take care of your hair is actually to take care of your scalp. Similarly, rather than simply taking pain meds to ease the ache, we can integrate healthy habits to tackle our health challenges.

Even small habits can affect your health and wellness. The toothbrush you use and the gum that you chew affect your teeth in the long-term. The shoes that you wear can add stress to your feet, knees, and back. Improving your hair care and personal hygiene can lift your mood and self-confidence. Maintaining your oral health and keeping regular dentist appointments allows you to have strong teeth, for longer. Adding a daily supplement to your routine can help you maintain muscle mass and improve your organ function. Over time, these small, healthy habits will shape your overall wellness. Through proactive and intentional interventions, you can transform your health now and safeguard your health for the future.

References for Future Learning

Abundance: The Future is Better Than You Think by Peter Diamandis and Steven Kotlers

Blowout Professor, YouTube channel by Chris Wenzel

Breath: The New Science of a Lost Art by James Nestor

Eat Smarter by Shawn Stevenson

Food Fix by Mark Hyman

Huberman Lab Podcast, a podcast by Andrew Huberman

Jaws by Sandra Kahn and Paul R. Ehrlich

Lifeforce by Tony Robbins

Lifespan: Why We Age—and Why We Don't Have To by David Sinclair

Limitless: Upgrade Your Brain, Learn Anything Faster, and Unlock Your Exceptional Life by Jim Kwik

MovementByDavid, a YouTube channel by David Thurin

Sleep Smarter by Shawn Stevenson

TheKneesOverToesGuy, a YouTube channel by Ben Patrick

Why We Sleep by Matthew Walker

CHAPTER 10

Gratitude

"The moment you trade your expectations for appreciation, your whole life will change."

—Tony Robbins

We've talked a lot about dreams, goals, and creation. Now, let's talk about the easiest way to live the most fulfilled life.

Be grateful.

As you continue on the path of personal growth, gratitude will become an important part of finding satisfaction and happiness. Author Hannah Whitall Smith once said, "The soul that gives thanks can find comfort in everything; the soul that complains can find comfort in nothing." The importance of gratitude hasn't changed over time. Greek philosopher Epictetus similarly said, "He is a wise man who does not grieve for the things which he has not but rejoices for the those which he has."

You can have everything in the world, but, without gratitude, will remain miserable. The inability to understand and appreciate the opportunities and blessings in your life will be a constant deterrent. While that's in the way, you'll never find greater peace or become comfortable with your place in the world.

Gratitude keeps you humble. It turns scraps into manna. It has far more power than the biggest sum of money in the world.

Every day, you wake up with the talents and time to improve yourself. You have the chance to create something positive. That's an opportunity to be grateful for.

The Power of Gratitude

Imagine that you give a child two cookies. The child jumps for joy—but then you take one of the cookies away. Still holding a cookie in their hand, most children will stay focused on the cookie that they lost. For some particularly stubborn children, they may even abandon the cookie they have in search for the cookie that they feel entitled to.

Compare this to a child who is given one cookie. The child jumps for joy. They eat their cookie.

While this example may seem elementary, it's important to acknowledge that both children, at the end of the day, have one cookie. Fixation on what you do not have drives you to misery. Of course, this is a natural human instinct. We try to protect our assets. However, this fixation means that our minds tend to dwell on what we've lost instead of what we've gained. What would you do if you woke up tomorrow morning with $40,000 in your bank account? How would you feel?

How would it affect you if somebody then stole something from you that was worth $20? Do you want to be the type of person who spends the other $38,980 trying to recover the $20 you lost, or are you going to spend that money in a more valuable way?

Without gratitude, we spend all of our time and energy on losses, past and present. We dedicate our lives to what we feel like our lives should have been. The irony is that this leads to more wasted time. Instead, we could be working towards a brighter future. When we look at our past experiences with gratitude, we're able to forgive—both ourselves and others. This gives us the power to embrace the past and move on.

So, if the child with one cookie is more grateful, does that mean we should prevent ourselves from seeking too much if we want to be happy? Not at all. The truth is, we're all the first child—there are things that all of us have lost, opportunities that we haven't had, problems that have poked holes in our dreams. It is our responsibility to retrain our minds to stop mourning what we've missed and start appreciating what we have. As John Ortberg says, "Gratitude is the ability to experience life as a gift. It liberates us from the prison of self-preoccupation."

Dr. John Demartini's book *The Gratitude Effect* is a must-read for anyone looking to enhance their happiness. It focuses on the power of gratitude for improving our daily lives. Dr. John uses insightful research and compelling personal anecdotes to explain that gratitude can increase our happiness, improve our relationships, and boost our overall well-being.

One of Dr. John's insights is the importance of being present and mindful. Being grateful improves our lives by helping us appreciate what we have as well as encouraging us to provide for others. Generosity and kindness are as much a product of gratitude as they can contribute to it. When we're grateful, we're more likely to express our appreciation for the people around us. Showing gratitude creates a loving environment that nurtures strong and meaningful connections. It also encourages us to be more empathetic and compassionate to others. When you are grateful for the support you receive, you're more likely to extend the same care for those around you. This doesn't just improve your personal relationships—this has the power to improve the world.

By shifting our focus from what we lack to what we have, we can develop a greater sense of perspective and better appreciate the lives that we live. In today's fast-paced and stressful world, gratitude is like a lifeline that maintains our focus (see Chapter 5) and shows us the joy in life's challenges.

Gratitude doesn't just generate powerful action—it changes who we are for the better. Practicing regular gratitude can actually rewire our brains. Gratitude boosts our mood and increases our mental health. It's like a booster shot for our emotional well-being. It can even reduce stress and give you a better night's sleep. That's right—gratitude has been associated with greater sleep quality and increased energy levels.

It also has the power to increase our self-esteem. When we practice self-gratitude, we get to recognize our own strengths. This affirming personal reflection boosts our confidence and enables us to face the world head-on. It also cultivates the abundance mindset, which can encourage us to remain optimistic and navigate difficult terrain. Ultimately, being grateful allows you to find joy in every day, no matter where you are in your personal journey. It can motivate you to take better care of yourself, maintain a positive mindset, and live a healthier and more fulfilling life.

Making Gratitude a Reality

Gratitude sounds great in theory, but anyone who's tried it knows that habitual gratitude isn't for the faint of heart. It requires us to shift our mindset and question our initial reactions. Anyone who's lived in a desert knows how to be grateful for rain. But how are you supposed to be grateful for the thunderstorm on your wedding day?

Those who are grateful as a habit are able to appreciate even the most challenging circumstances. Think back to our conversation on perspective (Chapter 2). Everything has a purpose. The world is beautiful when you're willing to look at it through your "grateful glasses." Maybe the rain is the only thing keeping the flowers on your front porch alive. Maybe the farmer next-door has been praying for a good downpour. Maintaining a grateful perspective through hardship is a necessity for finding long-term fulfillment. After all, would you rather hate the rosebush for having thorns or appreciate the thornbush for having roses?

Here are some helpful tips that I have discovered in my life to improve gratitude. These are a valuable place to start, but be sure to look up advice from other experts.

Keep a journal. So far, I've already discussed how journaling and similar habits can help you engage in self-reflection and maintain a positive outlook. Journaling can also be an excellent tool for developing gratitude. Make a goal to write down something that you are grateful for every day. If you want to increase gratitude in your relationships, consider making it a team effort. Both you and your partner make it a daily habit to record one thing about the other that you appreciate. Then, after both journals have been filled, trade them. These journals will act as a helpful reminder to you and your partner about the things you both do that benefit your relationship.

Count your blessings. When you feel discouraged, take a moment to think through all of the things that benefit your life. This can be your job, the people around you, and your past experiences. Be sure to note the little stuff—the air conditioning, a favor from a friend.

Practice generosity. Giving to others brings an appreciation for what you have. When you see others benefit from your accomplishments, you gain a better understanding of how actions big and small affect the world around you. Consider donating to charitable organizations or volunteering to help those in need.

But what about your boring work, or your labor-intensive job? How are you supposed to be grateful for that?

When you focus on the rewarding aspects of your work, such as the skills you are developing, the networking opportunities, and the impact you are making in the company, you can begin to feel more satisfied and fulfilled. This gratitude builds up into a sense of purpose and motivation, which can improve your work environment and even open professional opportunities for you. That's right—being grateful can even lead you to a job that more closely matches your personal goals.

Still, how can you be grateful for your power struggles with your thoughtless teenager?

Gratitude attracts peace. When you choose to be grateful for the challenges and tests that life throws at you, you allow the experiences to make you a better person. Being thankful for your experiences allows you to forgive those around you, whether you're struggling with a child or a colleague.

Besides, having gratitude for the opportunity to improve means that you will *actually* improve. You'll become more patient with your child, develop better communication skills, and establish a role model for conflict resolution.

In both personal and professional contexts, gratitude builds trust and respect, creates more fulfilling connections, and faces setbacks head-on. These are necessary if you want to create an environment of positivity and mutual respect.

Maintaining Gratitude and Drive

Does that mean gratitude fixes everything? Definitely not. Being grateful is essential to fulfillment and humility—but you'll want to be careful. Gratitude easily turns into contentment. If we only focus on what we have, we lose our drive for more. This may lead to missed opportunities as contentment rolls into negligence.

Be grateful, but never idle. You've only got so much fuel in your tank—if you idle too long, you may not end up as far as you want to be. Instead, use your gratitude to add fuel to the fire. It will encourage you to go farther and live as a powerful force for good.

References for Future Learning

The Gratitude Effect by Dr. John Demartini

CHAPTER 11

Taking Action

"Taking massive action on a less-than-perfect plan is better than planning for the rest of your life with no action."

You can study baseball for years. You can memorize every technique in the book. But you'll never hit a home run until you step up and bat. Everything great that has ever been achieved in the history of the world has one thing in common: the first step.

It's wonderful to have a good plan—but it's even better to have a good plan that's been put in action. Imagine putting two great ideas on opposite sides of a scale. The scales will always tip in favor of the idea that's been executed. It's only once you've put your ideas into action that they can affect the world. Execution will outweigh inaction every time.

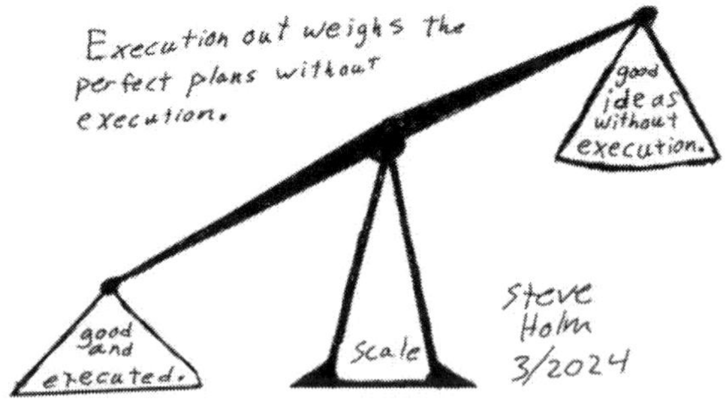

In this book, we've had a lot of philosophical discussion. We've gone on about making personal change, adjusting our mindsets, and growing our knowledge. In this chapter, we're going to address making movement. We're next in the lineup—now, we're ready to swing. Let's talk about taking action.

Goals Drive Action

Action begins with your brain, no matter how small the decision. If you decide that you want to turn a page in a book, the neurons in your brain begin firing, transmitting the directive through your nerves to your muscles. This all happens at lightning speed. In a split second, a thousand complex exchanges wire through your body to tell the right muscles to move. Then, you turn the page.

It's the same for big action. You have to start with your strategic vision. The bulk of the work should go into planning, coordinating, and setting the stage. This requires us to envision our future, develop goals, and create a detailed strategy (see Chapter 4).

Compared to the planning process, taking action can seem straight-forward. However, particularly for deep thinkers, it can be incredibly tempting to live in anticipation of actions that you never execute.

Overcoming Procrastination and Fear

If you're a procrastinator, chances are that you use tomorrow like a toxic habit. We love to push things to tomorrow, or an hour from now, or ten minutes from now. It takes the edge off. If we have something stressful on our plate, it's easier to put it on some ideal future version of ourselves that will be able to finish it perfectly in half the time.

Procrastination does a disservice to the actions that you might have made. When you take advantage of all the time that you have—instead of the time that you think you may "need"—you'll find that you might surprise yourself. You could have the potential to outshine all of the expectations, but you'll never find it if you let procrastination limit you.

To break through procrastination, it's important to get to its root cause. Though it may seem contradictory, procrastinators are often perfectionists. They want what they do to turn out perfect—so they get stuck in analysis paralysis.

Analysis paralysis occurs when you are overwhelmed by overthinking. You're centered on completing an action. Yet, you're so obsessed over the action that you've become frozen. It can feel like the situation is too complicated (it's not). It seems like there are too many factors to consider (there isn't). It looks like it's already too late to do anything about it (it never is). However, as a result of this paralysis, many issues can worsen. It's like you're hiking on a snowy day and you have to choose which way to go on a forked trail. You're paralyzed by the choice—but the snow is still coming down. By the time you start moving, there's an extra six inches on the trails.

Possible roadblocks are a massive component of analysis paralysis. If you have over-exercised your strategic vision, you may find that you're fixated on roadblocks six miles down the road. If you're not careful, you'll find yourself unmoving at home, waiting for all of the stoplights on the way to turn green before you even leave the driveway.

There are many different ways to fight procrastination. Some people swear by making false deadlines for themselves—others create a detailed schedule with smaller milestones to overcome their procrastination. In the next segment of this chapter, we're going to discuss some important points for killing your procrastination and ending your analysis paralysis.

Developing Action Steps

Your goals cannot be achieved by someone else. When you choose to become the master of your life, what you give is what you get. Your entire life is made up of everything we have chosen to do or ignored. You end up with the cumulative actions of everything you have ever done. The more good you do, the better your life becomes. If you don't do much, your life won't have much in it.

That means that the more action you take towards your goal, the faster you'll reach it.

Let's break it down. Here are some specific steps to developing action steps so that your goals don't end up stuck in the dream stage.

Start Small

In many instances, you can't begin with big action. Let's say you have a goal to start a business. Your first milestone is to get a business loan. But, before you can do that, you have to build your credit. This requires several small actions that aggregate over time.

It's like trying to lose weight. A weight loss goal of 50 pounds can seem overwhelming, and, often, impossible. But shedding 50 pounds isn't one action that is taken. It's several small decisions, every day, over the course of weeks and months.

Even small actions have the power to streamline your life and move you forward. I have a rule for myself. If there's something I need to do that will take less than two minutes to complete, I'll do it immediately. Sending an email, making the bed in the morning, apologizing to a friend—these are all small actions that, when done and checked off my to-do list, can help me make progress in the future.

Ultimately, committing to small actions reduces the strain that comes with committing to massive actions. It's easier to climb a step on a ladder than it is to jump a fence. Set small, achievable goals, and meet them with small actions. With time, these actions will make a positive impact in your life and ultimately bring you closer to your end goal.

Check Your Habits

A good habit is one of the most valuable investments you can have. Since they're second-nature, habits don't require much upkeep, but they have the power to transform your life just as much as intentional action. While you're developing action steps, be sure to consider the habits that you currently have. Which of those habits will enable you to reach your goal? What habits do you need to succeed? From there, you can begin to maximize your positive habits and reduce your negative tendencies.

Creating habits is like trying to get through a dense book. You begin by reading one paragraph. By committing to this small action, you've given yourself a leg up. Starting is often the most difficult step. From there, if you push yourself one paragraph at a time, you'll find that you've read a full page. Once the first page is done, you can set a goal to finish the first chapter. If you make this a daily habit, pretty soon, you'll be looking at the acknowledgements at the end.

Consider ways to replace negative habits with more proactive behaviors. Say you spend too much time doom-scrolling on social media. Every time you pick up your phone, train yourself to open an online book or news outlet instead. If Snapchat isn't actually improving your life, you're the only one who can toss it out. Using a crutch that you don't need doesn't just slow you down—it keeps you from developing muscles that you need to run. Luckily, there's plenty of additional advice out there for breaking bad habits. Don't limit yourself to what you find in this section. Take some time to stalk the internet for more advice on forming good habits.

Prioritize Self-Reflection

When I read *The Millionaire Fastlane* by author and entrepreneur MJ DeMarco, I had one main takeaway. I learned that there's a crucial difference between the fast lane and the slow lane. In the fast lane, small incremental changes can completely throw off your trajectory.

When you decide to become a driven, engaged individual, you can get in a focused headspace. You've done the strategizing and goal-setting that we've talked about earlier, so you're ready to get stuff done. However, as you start making progress, it can be difficult to track your trajectory. You don't have to leave the fast lane—but you'll want to keep an eye on even the smallest changes that you make. Live intentionally and reflect often to make sure that you stay on course.

Be Kind to Yourself

Remember that progress takes time. You have to be patient as well as persistent. To keep yourself motivated, celebrate your successes, learn from your failures, and remember that even small actions take you in the right direction.

Building Confidence Through Action

Confidence opens doors that you don't even know exist. You need confidence in every walk of life, from business to family and everything in between. The way that you hold yourself and view yourself will influence how others in your life view you.

This isn't anything new. But what does confidence have to do with action?

It's tempting to believe the common narrative that confidence is something that you are either born with or not. Many people think of confidence as some special quality that you can't really nail down.

In reality, confidence is like a muscle. It can be trained, and it has to be exercised to be maintained. Like muscles, confidence grows the more you use it.

About a month ago, I was driving with a friend about my age. He said, "The biggest difference that I notice between you and other people is your confidence."

"What do you mean?" I asked.

"You just give the vibe out that you are confident in what you are doing and saying," he explained. "You don't make us wonder where you stand in the room."

The secret to my confidence? Action.

Blair Enns's book *The Win Without Pitching Manifesto* has been a fantastic asset for building my confidence. Blair teaches us about assuming responsibility over our identity instead of relying on others to create our self-perception. This is the reason that the "fake it 'til you make it" model for building confidence actually works. It's about tricking your mind into believing that you have confidence, which inspires action. Then, that real action contributes to real confidence.

Action creates satisfaction, which creates confidence. By taking action and seeing the results of our hard work, we can begin to develop a stronger foundation for our self-perception. We begin to believe that we are capable because we've already proven it to ourselves. Once you've got a few successes under your belt, you're more likely to crush future opportunities with your newfound confidence. It feeds back into itself in a positive loop that increases both your capacity and your belief in that capacity. "Say less and do more" is a useful mantra for increasing personal confidence.

I once spent an extra $10,000 on wheels, tires, and customized details on a company truck. Every time I saw it, it served as a personal reminder to me of the work that I put in to earn these benefits. You need your own metaphorical reminder of what you have accomplished. It doesn't have to be something that you bought, and, if it is, it doesn't have to be expensive. It does, however, have to be a testament to your previous hard-earned rewards. These will encourage you to remember the power of your actions and give you the confidence you need to act.

Plan to meet your goals. Take action. Build your confidence. It's your future—it's time to make it a reality.

References for Future Learning

The Win Without Pitching Manifesto by Blair Enns

The Millionaire Fastlane by MJ DeMarco

CHAPTER 12

Balancing Life

"Life is about balance. Be kind, but don't let people abuse you. Trust, but don't be deceived. Be content, but never stop improving yourself."

—Zig Ziglar

At this point, you're familiar with many of the essential concepts that you'll need in your self-growth journey. You've got your feet planted firmly on the path. You're ready to seize control of your life, turn your dreams into tangible goals, and create real change in the world. It's time to become a better communicator, make healthy habits, create a financial plan, and develop a positive mindset.

Before you go, there's one last crucial concept that you'll need: balance.

Let's start with a visualization.

Begin by drawing a circle and then dividing it into sixths. Give each section a label: one for relationships, one for finances, one for mental health, one for physical health, one for spiritual health, and the final section for hobbies. These sections represent different elements of your life.

Now, give each section a score out of ten. This score reflects how much energy you put into that aspect of your life. So, for example, an 8/10 in your mental health would show that you put a significant amount of your energy into maintaining your mental wellness, while a 1/10 shows that your mental health is not a priority for you.

Then, shade in the section to reflect your score. A higher score should fill in more of the section.

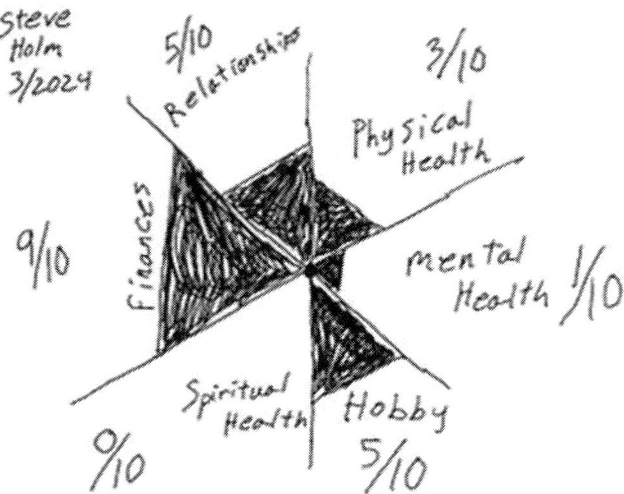

As you can see in the illustration above, this person has a 5/10 in relationships, 9/10 in their finances, 1/10 in their mental health, 3/10 in their physical health, 0/10 in their spiritual health, and 5/10 in their passion projects and hobbies. This indicates that their life is out of balance, as the vast majority of their effort is focused on their finances.

Now, imagine that this illustration is a wooden tire. The center of the circle is the hub, and the edges of the shaded sections make up the circumference. Think about using the tire in the illustrated example above. With so little effort expended on spiritual and mental health, it would be awkward—to say the least—to drive with this tire on your front axle. It's a rocky ride, with painful ups and downs as the tire spins from one section to the next. And it's not just uncomfortable—it's unsustainable. Chances are, the tire would get stuck in every rut in the road. Under any amount of pressure, you'd end up completely immobile.

What does your tire look like? Is it jagged or is it even? How would your tire hold up after a few miles? What section might cause you to stop?

To make progress on the road, you need a balanced tire, just like you need a balanced life to make progress in your personal journey.

Those who cultivate hunger and drive can become so committed to making their life extraordinary that they forget to live it. That's why balance is so important for reaching self-fulfillment.

Seeking True Fulfillment

Once, my brother was talking to an older mentor who was somewhere in his 70s. This man was incredibly rich. He owned several million dollars' worth of farmland. For those at the start of their financial journey, this man was living the dream. But, even with all the money he had, he was still missing a livelihood. He was lacking essential elements of life. He told my brother that he would trade all of his wealth and influence for a normal life with a purpose—with something to make him want to get up in the morning. He craved excitement and drive.

This is a result of an unbalanced life. His relationships, spiritual wellness, and mental health were running low. Even though he was fulfilled in other areas of his life, this lack of balance prevented him from finding happiness. His wheel was stuck in a mire.

In his book *Life's Amazing Secrets,* Guar Gopal Das provides a roadmap for living an authentic, purpose-driven life filled with joy and meaning. Guar's secrets to life don't just focus on success and financial gain. He writes about the power of self-awareness, passion, purpose, gratitude, positivity, and finding true meaning and authenticity. He speaks on the significance of cultivating strong relationships with others and the role of human connection in navigating the complexities of modern life.

This is tied into the Japanese concept of ikigai. Roughly, ikigai is a reason for being or an essence of life. Ikigai is made of four elements: what one loves, what one is good at, what the world needs, and what one can be paid for. It suggests that true happiness and fulfillment are found only when a person maintains all four elements. It's believed that discovering and pursuing one's ikigai leads to a happy and purposeful life. Inversely, seeking only one of these elements can lead to dissatisfaction.

It's important not to get caught up in the fantasy of success. You may want $1 billion, but that will never be everything that you need. It will not fulfill you. Balancing the different aspects of life in a manageable way will always give you more long-term benefits than excelling in only one area.

One day, Amy Sprouse, a holistic health educator, told me that she felt stuck in a battle between wanting to enjoy the world and wanting to make the world a better place. Those who are driven are often the most likely to suffer from this paralyzing problem. People who are committed to improving the world can quickly get burnt out. They're under the pressure of overwhelming loads and feel a lack of appreciation and recognition. Balance can prevent this burnout and increase our enjoyment of our current world, even while we dream of a better one. We must choose to invest in passion, in spiritual health, in relationships, and in emotional connection if we want to realize our vision for the future. It is the only sustainable way to make our dreams a reality.

Furthermore, it's nearly impossible to reach your full potential if your life is out of balance. Relationships give you connection, belonging and understanding. Healthy finances are a valuable tool for achieving goals and securing personal comforts. Quality mental health practices improve your clarity, your resilience, and your productivity. Good physical health enhances your overall quality of life. Spiritual health offers you purpose and meaning. Even your hobbies and passion projects help you grow in new ways by supporting creativity and innovation. In turn, your relationships can boost your physical health, just like financial stability may improve your mental health. Each aspect leans on the others. You will never be able to achieve your best in one area of your life if you're ignoring the rest.

Spiritual Health

While we've addressed many of the elements in our wheel, spiritual health is something that we've only briefly touched on so far. We've talked about developing our personal relationships, managing our physical and mental health, and getting our finances in order—now, let's get into caring for our spiritual wellness.

Spirituality gives us a sense of purpose, meaning, and connection. Without a belief in something greater, life is nothing. As Pierre Teilhard de Chardin said, "We are not human beings having a spiritual experience. We are spiritual beings having a human experience." Our spiritual connection is related to our sense of drive. For many, the desire to improve comes from a spiritual place. It encourages us to become better people and to improve the lives of others. Often, we find a sense of responsibility for our fellow human beings in our religious beliefs. Caring for others provides us with spiritual strength. As we discussed in Chapter 10, we build ourselves up when we give to others.

Over time, our spiritual growth will lead us to lasting peace. To me, there is comfort in knowing that God built the world for me to live in. The Bible tells us that God created all men, all beasts, all fowls of the air, and the land and water that we walk upon and swim in. You may think of it as a different deity, an unknown spirit, or just the universe at large—but whatever you call it, it's important to have a developed idea about your place in the world.

Our spiritual compass allows us to see beyond what we think is possible. French philosopher Voltaire wrote, "Faith consists in believing when it is beyond the power of reason to believe." Our beliefs are there to support us when fear tells us that hope is lost.

Faith, Not Fear

Faith, whether religious or internal, provides the strength and courage that we need to face our challenges. Faith is a belief in something hopeful. It's all about trust and positivity. Hebrews 13:6 reads, "Let your faith be bigger than your fear."

Fear exists to protect us from harm, so it's centered on doubt and negativity. While it does save us in dangerous situations, it can also prevent us from taking advantage of opportunities. When we're paralyzed by anxiety, we're allowing fear to override our faith.

On the other hand, faith has a built-in optimistic outlook. As French philosopher Voltaire wrote, "Faith consists in believing when it is beyond the power of reason to believe." Where fear hesitates, faith acts. It fosters an environment where our dreams can flourish, and then makes space for the action that we need to see it through. Faith isn't just praying for rain. It's bringing an umbrella on your walk.

One of the secrets to self-actualization is centering your faith over your fear. We can accomplish this by making our spiritual health a priority. Here's some advice for those looking to build up their sense of spirituality—consider this a jumping off point for your future research.

Explore different practices. Take time to research different spiritual traditions. Try a variety of routines, such as meditation and prayer. Seek spiritual advice from unexpected venues—some of the best spiritual advice can even be found online. Find what resonates with you and incorporate it into your daily routine.

Reflect. Spend time in quiet contemplation. Be committed to connecting with your inner self and fundamental beliefs.

Connect with nature. For many, time spent in nature can be a spiritual experience. Take walks, go hiking, or simply sit outside and appreciate the beauty of the natural world.

Engage in acts of kindness. Showing compassion to others can make you feel more connected to your humanity. It also cultivates a sense of purpose and fulfillment.

Seek a community. Connect with like-minded individuals who share your values. Join a spiritual community or attend religious meetings to surround yourself with those who support you in your spiritual journey.

When we build our spiritual health, we increase our positivity and determination, all while bringing lasting balance to our lives.

Keeping Hobbies

Hobbies or passion projects are another important element on our wheel. Passion projects, hobbies, and vacations are an important part of work/life balance.

But you might be thinking—this entire book has been about developing drive, pursuing goals, and maintaining focus. Why would we waste an entire section on hobbies?

Hobbies play an important role in your life. They can be a way for you to unwind and relax, reducing your overall stress and anxiety. Pursuing passion projects can also help you in your self-growth journey. You may discover new skills, explore untapped talents, or challenge yourself in exciting ways. Your hobbies can stretch your mental muscles in new directions, encouraging you to think outside the box and explore new ideas. The resulting accomplishment develops your confidence and sense of self. Plus, hobbies provide you with the opportunity to connect with others and build meaningful relationships in your community.

However, I would recommend that we re-evaluate how we think about our hobbies. If we remain fixated on these kinds of activities for fulfillment and happiness, we may ignore the joy that we can get from our everyday lives.

About six months ago, I went to a meeting where someone asked me about my hobbies. My answer went something like this—"What do you mean? My life is my hobby."

I have worked hard to create a life that I don't want to escape from. Because of that, I find joy in my day-to-day routine. I don't rely on side hobbies to get the happiness that I want. You can incorporate many of the joys from hobbies into your current lifestyle. When you treat your work in this way, you still get to enjoy your hobbies—you just get to be paid for them.

Similarly, vacations can be a valuable way to unwind, but relying on them for your dopamine kick won't get you anywhere. If you're fixated on your paid time off, you waste energy daydreaming about an escape instead of building a happier life. Put your energy to good use. A great life will last way longer than even the best vacation.

I'm certainly not saying that there's no time for vacations or side projects. But I would recommend that we think about what we really want when we pursue these kinds of activities. Do you need a full week's vacation, or do you really just need a 10-minute FaceTime with a friend to unload your stress and express your appreciation? Are you looking for a cross-country road trip, or do you actually just need a trip to the coffee shop?

When we're able to approach hobbies and passion projects with this perspective, we're able to prevent ourselves from pouring too much of our energy and time into these pursuits. At the same time, we're able to get the benefits that come with them. Toeing this line helps us to find the balance that we need.

Implementing Balance

Albert Einstein is credited with saying, "Life is like riding a bicycle. To keep your balance, you must keep moving."

You can't just think your way to a balanced life. It's not achieved by philosophizing in a chair. Balance requires work. You must be willing to put real, long-term effort into the neglected areas of your life. I have one piece of advice if you want to balance out the missing elements of your life: research.

There's a reason I've mentioned continual education several times throughout this book. It's incredibly important. Your future research contains secrets that may change your life.

Let's take another look at your wheel. What aspect has the lowest score? No matter what the concept is, there are hundreds of books out there that can help you improve in that area. The manuals are available. All you need to do is find them—and, through my recommendations, you already have a head start.

Beyond that, there are thousands of videos and webpages dedicated to the concepts that I've outlined in this book. Technology is a tremendous resource. You can find pretty much anything online. Hundreds of experts have published their personal experiences for all to see—completely free. Leverage the online space to become smarter. Fall down valuable internet rabbit holes. Subscribe to inspirational YouTubers. Use your online presence to improve yourself.

While you learn, apply the valuable concepts that you come across. Begin integrating life-changing advice as soon as you come across it. You'll find that the investment in your personal education immediately pays off.

Building Emotional Homes

How many times have you seen a news reel of a city being devastated by a natural disaster? Cyclones and tsunamis are commonplace in certain areas of the world. Every few years, these areas get hit by a massive storm that wipes out homes, damages infrastructure, and even threatens lives. After the storm has passed, the residents rebuild their homes, repair the area, and try to recreate their previous comforts—only for another storm to hit two years later. Why don't these people move to a safer place where they can build a house that lasts?

It's because that area is not just where they live. It's their home. Their home is what they know, and it would take far more than a cyclone to make them want to leave.

Human beings tend to earnestly seek a place to call home, both physically and emotionally. We're going to focus on emotional homes. A while ago, I discovered an essential idea from Tony Robbins. "Most people, about half of what they thought today is the same things they thought yesterday," he said. "About themselves, about their life, about their business. That's why most people's lives don't change very much. But if you woke up and started realizing, 'I'm living in an emotional home I don't want,' you can change it."

Look at emotional homes this way. Your emotional home is made of the habitual emotions that you keep returning to. It doesn't matter if you're a billionaire—if your habitual emotions are those of frustration and worry, then you live a frustrated and worried life. If that's your emotional home, you will always find your way back. They're an integral part of our mental health. An untended emotional home has the power to throw our entire life out of balance.

All of us have an emotional home. Usually, our emotional homes are shaped by our environment. Those who grew up in a brutal culture may naturally build a brutal emotional home. Even though it doesn't feel good, it feels comfortable, so this negative emotional space is one that we keep returning to.

If you're feeling unsuccessful, unfulfilled, and undriven, it may be that your emotional home is in need of some serious renovations. Maybe your emotional home is one of worry, of frustration, of anger, and of victimization. Though they may be influenced by our environment, we have the power to take responsibility for our own emotional homes. We can choose to make it a beautiful place to live. When we decide to cultivate peace and stability in our life through balance and reflection, we can analyze the structure of our emotional home and take action to improve it.

Are you ready to rebuild your emotional home? Invest in good habits and create a worthwhile life. Hold yourself to happiness. Live a balanced life, experience each moment fully, and break free of the limitations that are keeping you from your goals.

Breaking Free of Limitations

Standing up, full-grown bulls are taller than the average man. On its own, a bull can weigh more than 2,000 pounds—literally, a ton. They're like living, breathing battering rams with built-in anger issues.

Yet you'll find that many bulls live fenced in by standard wire netting. Why wouldn't the bulls just barrel through the flimsy fence towards freedom?

The answer: the bull grew up in the fence. When it was first born, it couldn't push the fence over. It conditioned its brain to think that it couldn't get through the wire, and then, when it was big enough to completely mow it over, it never even tried.

This is the flea-in-a-jar mindset. When fleas are put in a jar with a lid, the fleas will start by flying furiously at the lid to escape. After hitting the lid enough times, the fleas learn that they can't escape, and they stop flying at the lid. Eventually, when the lid is removed, the fleas will stay in the main body of the jar. Essentially, they have learned to limit themselves based on past experiences.

Like the bull and the fleas, we also condition ourselves to believe in limitations based on previous experience. This is in an attempt to protect ourselves, of course—no use cutting ourselves on a fence or bruising ourselves on a lid—but it means that we often end up with self-imposed limitations. These hold us back from the experiences that we want.

As we finish our discussion on balance, I want you to remember the images of the barely-fenced bull and the fleas stuck in the open jar. We often choose to ignore the aspects of our lives that don't come easy to us—the ones that have hurt us or discouraged us in the past. Remember that both you and your circumstances are subject to change. Don't live in an unbalanced state because you're sure that the way is closed, or that you're not strong enough to push through to the other side. Believe in yourself. Test your limits. Be willing to improve in the areas where you struggle. Balance is an option. You are worth the effort it will take to get there.

To me, a happy life is one that's lived on your own terms. It's built around constant learning and continual improvement. It's a balance of never being content with staying where you're at while always being grateful for how you got to where you are. I want a life with a healthy body and a wealthy spirit, filled with both drive and appreciation. This balance is the key to living a life full of discipline, joy, and fulfillment.

References for Future Learning

Life's Amazing Secrets by Guar Gopal Das

Conclusion

The Lord has given us flour, eggs, milk, pans, and a functioning oven, but he's rarely—if ever—given us cake. Similarly, God has told us that we can have happiness, but He won't force it on us. All He'll do is give us the recipe. If we want happiness, we still have to put the leg work in.

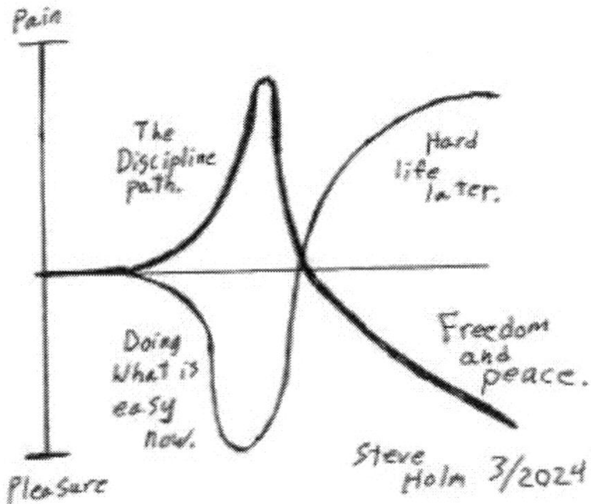

One day, I was talking with a friend of mine. Together, we drew the graph illustrated above. The horizontal axis represents time. The vertical axis on this graph represents the level of discomfort that we have to endure. Above the horizontal axis, we're in pain territory. Below, we're in pleasure. The higher up on the vertical axis that we go, the more pain.

So, we have two lines on the graph: the easy path, and the path of discipline. Both lines start in the center of the vertical axis. However, as time passes, the easy path dips down towards pleasure. Those who take the easy path want to do what is easy now. Though the easy path endures less pain in the early phase of life, it quickly climbs the chart over the course of time. When we choose an easy life now, we're also choosing a harder life later.

The other line, the path of discipline, is a mirror image. It spikes up in pain and effort early on. Then, as the rewards start to come in, the path of discipline gradually becomes easier, eventually leading to freedom and peace. When we sacrifice for our present, we're able to enjoy a peaceful future.

In this life, you'll only be as happy as you are willing to become. You're a winner. You don't need excuses. Nurture beneficial characteristics. Self-discipline, a positive mindset, strategic planning, and continuous learning are a surefire recipe to getting what you want. Commit, and then remain committed. Remember that you're involved in a constant battle. Every morning, from the moment your alarm clock goes off, the war is on. So, are you winning the war? Or are you in constant retreat?

Lewis Caralla, football coach and author, said, "Lazy people do a little work and think they should be winning. Winners work as hard as possible and still worry if they're being lazy." We should strive to embody this level of drive. It's time to go out and live a beautiful life on our terms. There's no use complaining about your circumstances. Life is what it is, but it will become what you make it.

We all know the hiking fanatic that climbs the mountain, turns around, hikes back down—and then goes back to climb it all over again. This is how we should be about seeking personal fulfillment. Our lives aren't just about the destination, they're about the journey. Continual challenge, improvement, and refinement should be our goal.

We're all climbing that mountain, though it looks different for each of us. Some want to hike the mountain the old-fashioned way—others may want to take a jeep and ride up the mountain side. Some people stick to the winding, paved road, even if it takes them longer to get there. The wild ones will just save up, buy a helicopter, and fly to the top. None of these methods are innately better than the others. It's all about setting your own pace, finding your own process, and enjoying your own adventure.

So, pick your route. Get started on your journey. We can never make our dreams a reality until we put forth the effort to reach them.

Eliminate Limiting Beliefs

Some of our most foundational beliefs are actually holding us back from making radical progress. We wait for the right time, even though there may never be a perfect time to begin. We want to do what's right. We obsess so much about what others think. We limit ourselves to our comfort zone instead of embracing the unknown. We get side-tracked from long-term fulfillment by short-term distractions.

At the heart of it, these limiting beliefs are based in a fear of failure. We worry about making mistakes. We avoid the things that matter. We're stuck in a sort of eternal stage fright.

So how do we overcome the fear of failure? First, acknowledge that everyone is afraid of failure. Fear is like a 100-foot-wide river that is 1-inch-deep. It's scary when you see it, just like it is when you see anything new. You have to start crossing the river, and you'll find that you're completely capable of handling the current.

Even if you do fail, you can use your experiences as the foundation for your future success. Failure doesn't have to be a setback—it can be a learning lesson that propels you forward. After you've failed, it can feel like you'll never recover—but the truth is that everyone who has ever found success found a lot of failure, first.

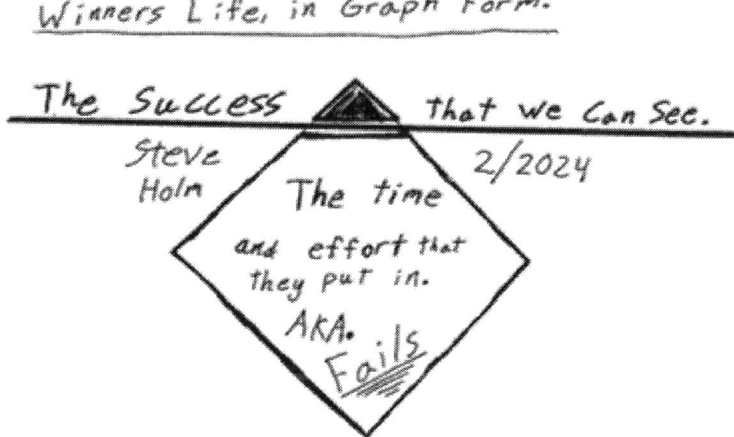

I call this illustration the Winner's Life. It's a rudimentary illustration of an iceberg. The tiniest tip of the iceberg that is visible represents success. When we look at winners, this is all that we see. However, most of the iceberg is hidden underneath the water. This represents the time and effort that winners put into their lives, including embarrassing failures, devastating setbacks, and challenging roadblocks. For most people, success doesn't come for free. If you watch for long enough, you'll find a heavy block of persistence hovering right below the surface.

Every person has challenges that they have to struggle with. If you ever met someone who doesn't have any problems in their life, you should call emergency services—you'll need to get their heart beating again. It's blunt but true; dead people are the only kind of people who don't have problems. Problems are part of life, and our reactions to them define who we are. When life knocks you on your knees, say a prayer, thank God for this beautiful life, and then get up and get going.

I know what it feels like to read an encouraging book and become inspired to reach your dreams, only to fall back into a depressing hole of reality. The hole locks you in—everywhere you turn, the walls are plastered with limiting ideas. *You can't do it. You're too young. You're too old. It's too late. It's too hard.*

You have the power to erase those signs and write new ones. After all, you're the one who put the first messages up on the walls. You can choose to broadcast the message that you enjoy the challenge. That you're here for the process. That you're determined to make everything better because you touched it.

I could waste all day telling you that you are loved, that you are beautiful, or that you'll be successful. But if, on the inside, you're determined to be unhappy, there's nothing that I, or anyone else, can do for you. On the other hand, if you're determined to succeed, then no one in the world can stop you from reaching your goals. True fulfillment comes from within—it can't be purchased with money or given by someone else.

You are well on your way to where you want to be. As you continue to teach yourself the art of growing and improving, you'll find that happiness and fulfillment will start coming into focus.

The vital lesson of this book is perfectly encapsulated in a beautiful song, "Improve the Shining Moments" by Robert B. Baird. I've included the main verses here:

Improve the shining moments;
Don't let them pass you by.
Work while the sun is radiant;

Work, for the night draws nigh.
We cannot bid the sunbeams
To lengthen out their stay,
Nor can we ask the shadow
To ever stay away.

Time flies on wings of lightning;
We cannot call it back.
It comes, then passes forward
Along its onward track.
And if we are not mindful,
The chance will fade away,
For life is quick in passing.
'Tis as a single day.

As wintertime doth follow
The pleasant summer days,
So may our joys all vanish
And pass far from our gaze.
Then should we not endeavor
Each day some point to gain,
That we may here be useful
And ev'ry wrong disdain?

Improve each shining moment.
In this you are secure,
For promptness bringeth safety
And blessings rich and pure.
Let prudence guide your actions;
Be honest in your heart;
And God will love and bless you
And help to you impart.

Facing the Future

As I've developed my vision for the future, I've known that I wanted to leave a legacy. I wanted to measure my success by the number of people I have blessed by the time I leave this world. Your popularity may rise and fall, but your legacy will live long after you go. Instead of trying to please the people who came before us, we should be forward-thinking. Don't be slave to traditions that don't serve you. Let's focus on creating a life that will benefit future generations.

Your actions will impact, either positively or negatively, the lives of those around you. Make connections with the intent of lifting others up. Approach future relationships with this mindset: the more people you know, the more people you can bless. This is how we shape a lasting legacy.

Three months ago, I woke up with something on my mind. It was a 2:50 AM thought—one of the ones I knew I would have to write down, or else I would forget it. I dreamed about an interview where I asked a few questions that I'd never asked anyone before:

Are your needs aligned with your goals? Are your goals aligned with what you truly need? Are they put into actionable steps?

If the answer to these questions is anything less than "yes," it may be time to revisit your goals and your vision for the future. If you ask yourself these questions regularly, you'll be sure to create a life that exceeds your every expectation.

Recommended Reading

As we wind down to the end of this book, I'd like to recommend some additional reading for your continuing education. Here are some of my favorite reads that have influenced my life—I think they will benefit yours.

The Holy Bible. Before 2000, over 5 billion copies of the Bible were printed. There's no better book to read. The principles in this book do not change, and you can relate the concepts you learn in every other book to what you learn here.

***The 5 AM Club: Own Your Morning, Elevate Your Life* by Robin Sharma.** This book emphasizes the importance of early mornings for providing us some quiet and focused time for self-improvement and reflection. It also dives into specific routines for harnessing energy, mindfulness, and knowledge, and developing self-discipline and fostering continual learning.

***Relentless: From Good to Great to Unstoppable* by Tim S. Grover.** This book was written by a personal trainer and is a guide to achieving mental and physical fitness. It's a great book if you can handle some tough love.

Additional books to tag on your reading list include:

The Speed of Trust: The One Thing that Changes Everything by Stephen Covey

The 3rd Alternative by Stephen Covey

The 8th Habit by Stephen Covey

Think Bigger: How to Innovate by Sheena Iyengar

The *Rich Dad, Poor Dad* book series by Robert Kiyosaki and Sharon Lechter

$100M Leads: How to Get Strangers to Want, and other books by Alex Hormozi

These books will provide some guidance for the next steps in your journey. Even if you consume all the content recommended in this book, you'll still just be dipping your toes into the world of personal improvement.

Live with Purpose

I believe in the tutoring effect. It's a psychology term that refers to the power of teaching. Often, in explaining concepts to others, the teacher learns.

In this way, this book was just as much for me as it was for you. I hope you've learned as much from it as I have.

I've been grateful for the opportunity to share my experiences and perspectives with you. I truly hope that my words have brought you inspiration and encouragement. When you close this book, you may be facing the moment that will ignite a revolutionary change in your life.

Live with passion. Live with purpose. Live every moment to the fullest. Never run life on idle.

Stay humble, and most of all, stay hungry—hungry to grow, to create, and to become more.

I really appreciate the time that you've given to this book. I hope that it's earned a quick review from you. Thanks again for your time.

May God bless you on your beautiful life journey!

Steve Holm

Made in the USA
Columbia, SC
06 October 2024

84aa2c6c-ccf6-4f1f-a127-7d61ffdba027R01